To the Back of Beyond

by the same author

EASTERN APPROACHES
DISPUTED BARRICADE
A PERSON FROM ENGLAND
BACK TO BOKHARA

To the Back of Beyond

An illustrated companion to Central Asia
and Mongolia

FITZROY MACLEAN

... to the back o' beyont
SIR WALTER SCOTT

JONATHAN CAPE
THIRTY BEDFORD SQUARE LONDON

ACKNOWLEDGMENTS

For their assistance with the preparation of the text my thanks are due to Mrs Clissold, Miss Thorburn, Mrs Cookson and Miss Wickham

SET IN 12PT GARAMOND 2 PTS LEADED

PRINTED IN GREAT BRITAIN BY
BUTLER AND TANNER, FROME AND LONDON

Contents

FOR JAMIE
who had been to Outer Mongolia
and back before he was out of
his teens

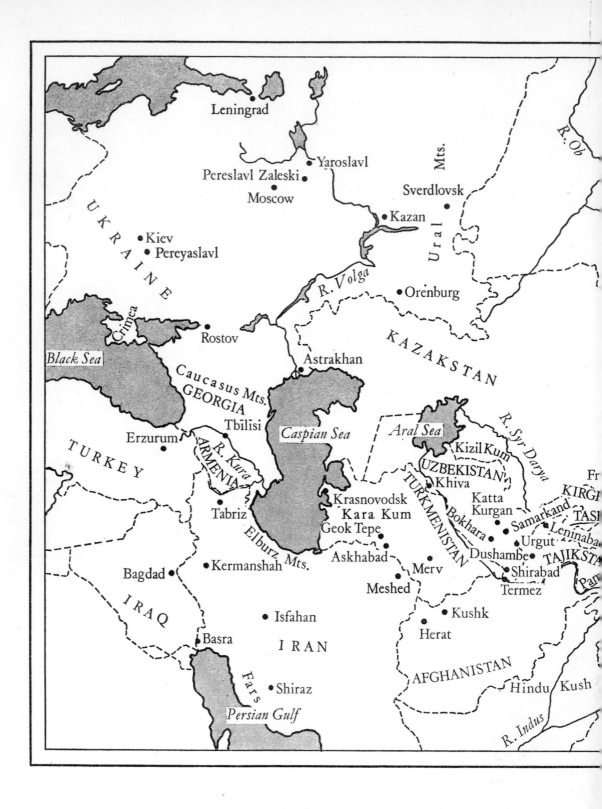

Foreword

This is neither a serious work of scholarship nor even a serious travel book. It simply represents the result of a certain amount of desultory reading and a good many years of equally desultory travel and photography in and around Central Asia. My chief excuse for publishing it is the more or less innocent amusement I have derived from writing and illustrating it and the hope that what I have written and the photographs I have taken may conceivably be of some interest to intending travellers in the regions I have described.

Strachur, Argyll   F. M.

And they know full well that men dwell there, but they know not what manner of men.

SIR JOHN MANDEVILLE

I *All the Russias*

To me the Soviet Union will always be one of the most fascinating countries on earth. Though I have been back a dozen times since I first went there over thirty years ago, each time I go back it is still an adventure: because you are going from one world to another completely different one.

When we speak of the Soviet Union, most of us are inclined to call it 'Russia' and its inhabitants 'Russians'. But more than half its territory lies in Asia, and, although admittedly the largest and most important, Russia is, in fact, only one of the fifteen different Soviet Socialist Republics of the Union, inhabited for the most part by people as different from European Russians as the people of Hong Kong or Bombay are from those of London or Birmingham.

The historical reason for this is that in the seventeenth, eighteenth and nineteenth centuries, while other European nations were founding colonies overseas, the Russians were busy expanding at the expense of their immediate neighbours, conquering vast new territories and incorporating them and their inhabitants within the all-embracing frontiers of their Empire. Siberia, Transcaucasia, Central Asia, all went the same way. 'All the Russias', wrote Gogol, 'the land which has spread smoothly, glidingly over half the earth.' And the Tsar was called 'Tsar of All the Russias'.

Vital in this was the plain – the limitless Russian plain, snow-covered in winter, muddy in spring and autumn, dusty and breathless in summer. The plain formed the Russian character and shaped the course of Russian history. To it can be attributed the autocratic character of successive Russian regimes. Historically, mountains have everywhere been the home of freedom and independence, while the dwellers in the plains have tended to fall under the rule of tyrants. If the Russians were to survive as a nation, a strong central authority was needed to keep them together and to weld them into a homogeneous whole, into a nation that could withstand the successive invasions of the Mongol and Tartar hordes that swept in from Asia, burning and pillaging as they came.

The plain has also had its effect psychologically. The flat expanse in which they live is, I suspect, at least partly responsible for the innate vio-lence of the Russians, for their explosiveness, their love of colour, their taste for drama and music and strong drink, for their moods and their melancholy. They needed to escape, from the weather and the cold and the bleak flatness stretching endlessly away under the grey dome of the sky. The plain, too, has surely contributed to the quality of which they them-selves are proudest, to the 'breadth' or 'generosity' of their nature. And, indeed, you can see how, if you lived in a plain that size, you might be inclined not to bother too much about details or distance or the passage of time.

Finally it was the plain, spreading temptingly away for thousands of miles in every direction, that gave the Russians their urge to expand. Once they had begun to consolidate their position, it was the obvious thing for them to do, to expand at the expense of those same Tartar hordes who had come charging down on them out of Asia; to expand across Siberia and across the Behring Strait into America; to expand eastwards or westwards, northwards or southwards, wherever the opportunity offered.

Most people nowadays have some idea of what European Russia is like. Even if they have not been to Moscow, they have seen pictures of the Kremlin with its pinnacles and palaces and spires and its profusion of strange treasure-trove: the great gun that never fires; the great bell that never rings; Peter the Great's gigantic boots; the cloak made for Catherine the Great from the feathers of a thousand orange parakeets; the Tsar's platinum model of the great Trans-Siberian express. They can recognize by now the vast expanse of Red Square, with the variegated onion domes of St Basil at one end, and, lying directly under the Kremlin wall, the squat dark basalt mass of Lenin's mausoleum. They are familiar, too, with the architectural fantasies of GUM, the immense arcaded State Department Store that lies across Red Square from the Kremlin and is today the epi-centre of a consumer revolution scarcely less radical than that other revo-lution of half a century ago. They know the Bolshoi Theatre. They have seen, till they are tired of them, Stalin's ornate wedding-cake skyscrapers, and, more lately, block upon endless block of new workers' tenements, stretching far out into the suburbs.

They have also come to know the classical magnificence of Leningrad, more western in concept and style, with its formal patterns of palaces and gardens and canals; the elegant façade of the Winter Palace and the great square that adjoins it; the Admiralty with its slender golden spire, and, across the swirling waters of the Neva, the matching golden spire of St Peter and St Paul; the vast dome of St Isaac's cathedral, with, in front of it, Peter the Great on his horse; and then, outside the city, the fantastic splendours of Peterhof and Pushkin and Pavlovsk.

They feel, too, that they know something of the Russian people: of their struggles and of the sufferings endured by them in successive wars, in the Revolution, and in Stalin's purges and counter-purges; of the gradual changes that, over the years, have been taking place in Russia, both in the life of the people, and even, within limits, in the character of the regime. The Russians, they know, are learning to think for themselves and are gaining in self-confidence. Their natural good nature and generosity and turbulence and gregariousness are again very gradually coming to the surface. The Secret Police, though still very much there when required, have, from their once dominant position, begun to some extent to fade into the background. Less obtrusive, too, is the 'cult of personality', the concentration of total, unlimited power in one man's hands. In Stalin's day, vast portraits of the Leader were everywhere. Today a not very inquisitive foreigner could spend several weeks in the Soviet Union without immediately identifying the Secretary General of the Communist Party, or consciously recognizing his likeness. The leaders of today are powerful, but not all-powerful. The resulting void has been filled, and more than filled, by the cult of Lenin. 'Lenin', say the gold letters on the banners and streamers and posters, 'is always with us.' 'Lenin is more alive than the living.' And it is absolutely true. The benign, bearded face gazes down at you from every wall and every street corner, infinitely avuncular and infinitely understanding. Politically speaking, there can be no doubt that a dead leader often has many advantages over a living one.

With time, a whole new society, with new values and a new, widely graduated class-structure, has come into being. 'Forward with Lenin to Communism', say the electric signs on the buildings and the banners in the processions, much as the Victorians, by texts, placards and exhortations from the pulpit, were reminded, with approximately the same impact, that the Kingdom of Heaven was at hand, or urged to prepare to meet their God. Superficially, there is much about the Soviet Union that is Victorian both in style and in spirit. There is the same prevailing self-confidence, not to say smugness. There is a new and powerful ruling class of politicians, officials, artists, scientists and technicians, captains of industry, generals and admirals, enjoying and consolidating their position and privileges, and, what is more, passing them on to their children: a class that you can see in strength on a gala night at the opera, or disporting themselves on the shores of the Black Sea. There is an altogether Victorian attachment to material standards and values, and a strong belief in human and material progress and in the unlimited human and material resources of an immense empire. There is, for most people, a gradually improving standard of living. There is, too, a nineteenth-century respectability, often verging on prudishness, and going hand in hand with a conviction that honesty is the best policy and a belief in hard work, especially for the working class. There is a deep-rooted, old-fashioned patriotism and a simple faith in their country's imperial mission and military strength. There is an increasingly patronizing attitude towards lesser breeds without the law and a growing uneasiness about the Yellow Peril. There are, finally, the new boarding schools where, away from the unsettling influence of home, the precept of *mens sana in corpore sano* is inculcated in the rising generation with a zeal worthy of Dr Arnold.

Of these solid virtues and no less solid values the outward and visible signs are everywhere: the massively ornate public buildings; the elaborate public parks, with their concrete colonnades, and pedestals supporting statues of nubile sports-girls, who, on closer inspection, prove to be not nude but decorously draped by some Soviet Mrs Grundy in plaster-of-paris panties; the solid mahogany furniture; the yards and yards of crushed plush; the solid Socialist realism of highly representational art and sculpture; the heavy crystal and bronze chandeliers; the great industrial installations; the endless rows of sensible tenements for the workers. All these provide a suitable background to an era of imperial and industrial expansion and consolidation.

But just as the Victorian age was also the age of Darwin and Swinburne, of Karl Marx at Highgate and the Prince of Wales at Tranby Croft, the age not only of missions and prayer meetings, but of champagne suppers at the Café Royal; not only of Kings and Emperors but of revolutionaries and anarchists; not only of simple faith, but of doubts and heresies; so today in the Soviet Union there are signs that, somewhere beneath the solid, pompous, confident exterior, something much less accountable is stirring, something that, in all its different manifestations, can best be defined as human nature.

At all levels of society (but especially at the top) a generation is growing up which knew not Stalin, a beat generation not interested in politics, believing, as the Russians say, 'in neither God nor Devil', in neither Yogi nor Commissar, believing chiefly in having a good time and finding out how foreigners do the twist (or whatever has taken its place). These are the young people you see in the bars and cafés and restaurants, drinking and living it up and shocking their elders and betters. Though possibly less significant than they themselves imagine, these beatniks, hippies, and, for the matter of that, spivs, and their female equivalents with their jeans, mini-skirts, platform shoes, new-style hair-dos and fishnet stockings, have by the mere fact of their existence and force of their example a very definite social and political significance. They are a leaven, a portent, a sign of what might be, and those in authority see this and shudder.

Among the Soviet intelligentsia, too, new ideas keep stirring, ideas which the powers that be find disturbing and against which they have reacted vigorously with trials, expulsions and prison sentences. But the intellectuals fight back with speeches from the dock and public protests in the street, with books and pamphlets and underground news-sheets. And, even in the climate now prevailing, it is hard to see how the new ideas can fail to win through in the end. For the days when a bullet in the back of the neck was the answer to everything are past. And so the authorities find themselves in a serious dilemma, and policy is delicately balanced between what must be grudgingly granted and what can still be safely withheld.

But perhaps the biggest revolution of all has been the consumer revolution. In Stalin's day everything — particularly the day-to-day needs of the people — was sacrificed to the Moloch of heavy industry. Life for the average Russian, as well as being terrifying, was as drab and as dreary as it could be. Now this is no longer so. There are still shortages. By comparison with the West there is still a poor choice of goods. But gradually the Russian consumer is coming into his own. His — and still more *her* — needs and tastes are increasingly taken into account. To meet the ever more insistent demand for a better standard of living, the whole balance of the Soviet economy is being altered. Today a market economy is in operation. Goods are produced because people want to buy them and not just to fulfil some theoretical norm. 'The urge to possess one's own car', wrote *Isvestia* some years back, 'is as compelling as technical progress itself.' And now, all over the Soviet Union, more and more privately owned cars are appearing on the streets, bringing to the individual citizen a new mobility and independence.

As a result of this consumer revolution, the Russians are better fed, better housed and better dressed, and have a wider range of goods to choose from. And, of course, like anyone else, the more they get, the more they want. Even the State shops are no longer the dreary places they used to be, and at Soviet fashion-shows the models and the girls who show them are beginning to have a genuine Paris flavour. No longer does the visiting foreigner stand out among a crowd of Russians like a canary amid a flock of sparrows. In Russia human nature, especially feminine human nature, is asserting itself and serving as an ever-stronger catalyst. Gradually, in all these ways, the barriers that divide us from the Russians, though still formidable, are becoming less so. Russia no longer seems as remote and mysterious as it did twenty years ago. By Western standards, things are slowly becoming more normal.

But when it comes to the non-Russian parts of the Soviet Union, the distant outposts and borderlands, most Westerners are on much less familiar ground. If these areas are not inhabited by Russians, they ask themselves, then who are they inhabited by? And what goes on there? What sort of life do the inhabitants have? Are they less Communist than the Russians, or more so? Less or more civilized? Less or more prosperous? Have they any sort of autonomy or independence? Or are they simply Russian colonies? Are they left to themselves, or ruled from Moscow? Has the loosening-up process reached them yet, or have they somehow got left out and left behind? It is with the object of trying to find answers to some of these questions, and of seeing things for myself, that from time to time I pack my bags and travel to some distant Soviet Republic.

My journeys, as often as not, have been by train. Trains, even in these days of champagne suppers served to soft music by trim air-hostesses at a height of 30,000 feet, still have a powerful appeal, for me at any rate: not so much the branch lines of British Railways as the great transcontinental expresses, thundering through the night with their precious load of diplomats, multi-millionaires, blonde countesses, confidence men and secret agents.

But for the ultimate in railway travel you must, to my mind, go to Russia, and on through Russia to Central Asia and Siberia, where you can travel by train for days on end until your fellow passengers and the conductor and the waitresses in the dining car have all become old friends. For Siberia is bigger than America or China and India together, and takes, from Moscow to the Pacific, the best part of ten days to cross, through a flat, scarcely varying landscape of endless plain and forest. Even the Ural

Mountains pass unnoticed. Indeed, if I had not once happened to stop off at the town of Sverdlovsk, which lies at their foot, I should never have seen them. Only Lake Baikal briefly breaks the monotony of the journey, with its vast expanse of waters among the surrounding wooded hills — the deepest lake, they say, in the world. And then, at intervals, the towns, today gigantic centres of industry and population which forty or fifty years ago were only overgrown villages, like the straggling groups of wooden shacks that you see every now and then from the train window.

For me all Soviet trains, whatever their destination, have enormous charm. I remember the first I ever saw. I joined it at what was then the Polish frontier, at Nyegoreloye, where in those days the narrow-gauge European track ended and the broad Russian one began. The carriage was not very new. It had been built thirty-four years earlier, in the year 1903. My compartment, I found, was tremendously spacious — higher and (owing to the broad gauge) wider than any I had ever seen. It was also terrifically ornate, figured velvet upholstery standing out from polished mahogany panelling and heavy wrought ormolu metalwork. The conductor, like the coach, was a survival from Tsarist days, a frail old man with long drooping moustaches. With trembling hands and immense deference of manner, he brought me clean sheets, a saucer of caviar, some black bread and half a tumbler of vodka. Presently the engine gave a long, wolf-like howl, quite unlike the cosy toot emitted by British locomotives, and we set out at a steady twenty-five miles an hour across the snow-covered plain towards Moscow and points east.

Since then I have travelled by train over most of the Soviet Union — sometimes more comfortably and sometimes less, for class distinctions in Soviet trains are sharply marked. In those days whole areas of the Soviet Union were forbidden to foreigners. To get where I wanted, I would board a train, bound, say, for Siberia, travel in it for two or three days, and then, when the right moment arrived, slip off it suddenly and unobtrusively and take another train to a point nearer to my ultimate target: and so on, until I eventually reached my destination. Sometimes the Secret Police would interfere and sometimes not. It was not a particularly comfortable way of travelling, involving, as it did, queueing for hours for tickets and food and sleeping on the populous platforms of remote Siberian or Central Asian railway stations, or in trucks jam-packed with a cross-section of all the different races in the Soviet Union. But one made a lot of friends and it was never boring.

Latterly, railway travel in the Soviet Union has changed in a number of respects. If he keeps away from rocket-sites and frontier zones, even a foreigner can now travel freely almost anywhere he likes. And the antiquated rolling stock of pre-war days has been replaced by handsome new grey-green coaches emblazoned with coats of arms. But there is much that has stayed the same: the atmosphere, first and foremost. It is at its most convivial in the 'hard' class. Here, with forty or more passengers to a carriage, stacked three deep on their narrow shelves, everyone soon gets to know everyone else. You can't stay strangers for long. Day and night, there are always people eating and drinking and talking and singing. At each stop there is a rush to get boiling water to make tea and to buy food from the peasants who assemble at the stations with their wares: eggs, bread, cooked chickens, sausages, cheese, sour milk, fruit, vegetables, and flowers, for all Russians love flowers. Then the train starts. Everyone piles back in to compare their purchases and share them out and hand them round. Someone produces some beer or a bottle of vodka. An accordion is brought out and you have the makings of a party.

Often the train stops long enough for you to be able to pick flowers or go for a walk, and it is quite usual for enterprising passengers to leap on the backs of any horses, or, in Central Asia, camels that happen to be grazing near the track and take a ride round. Once, near Sochi, we all stripped to our underpants and dived, men, women and children alike, into the Black Sea, to be summoned, a quarter of an hour later, back to our carriages, dripping wet, by a long-drawn wail from the engine.

In the 'soft' coaches, where there are only four passengers to a sleeping compartment, things are a little quieter. 'I am so important', a travelling official once said to me sadly, 'that now I have to travel soft. You can't think how I miss the fun in the hard coaches. Why, I might even be all alone in my compartment!' But in Russia even four passengers, usually of mixed sexes, are a party in themselves. Small children, drifting up and down the passage and in and out of the doors, help people to make friends. The news that there is a foreigner on the train brings people crowding in from neighbouring compartments. Bottles of brandy or champagne come out, and soon you are well away.

For anyone who values true magnificence, the 'luxury'-class carriages are the ones to go for. Returning after the war, I was afraid that in the new coaches all the crushed plush and polished mahogany of which I had such happy memories would have vanished. Far from it. There was more than ever, together with a new abundance of cut glass, bronze and brass. The curtains, which button, are of thick red velvet. On the floor there is a Bokhara carpet. The steam-heating is hidden behind a heavily chased ornamental bronze grille. On the little table stands a brass lamp with a bright green silk shade. At the end of the passage is a fine big samovar from which the conductor dispenses endless glasses of hot sweet tea in ornamental metal holders. For breakfast, which one has in bed, there are piping-hot *piroshki*, crisply fried golden-brown savoury *beignets*, brought round in a basket wrapped in a clean white napkin.

In this rarefied atmosphere, it is true, relations are more formal. But soon everyone is bowing and wishing each other good morning and good night, and in the corridor gracious acquaintanceships grow up between the travelling generals and high officials and their female counterparts. The smart thing to wear on Soviet trains and station platforms is a suit of brightly striped pyjamas, put on over one's everyday clothes, and this in itself lends an air of pleasing informality to the proceedings.

Finally, there is the dining car, with, sometimes, if you are lucky, caviar, borsch, sturgeon, and *bœuf Stroganov*, and sometimes a more restricted menu. But, variable though the food may be, Soviet dining cars are friendly places. Once, seeing that I was reading *Anna Karenina*, the head waiter sat firmly down opposite me. 'Do you think she was right to behave as she did?' he asked. 'Or wrong?' And we had a most enjoyable discussion, while everyone waited for the next course.

Trains, as poor Anna found to her cost, play an important part in Russian life. They provide the perfect background for so many things the Russians value: warmth, and human contacts and gregariousness, and eating and drinking, and long, long conversations. I hope they will continue to do so. You can cross Siberia by jet in a few hours, where a train takes as many days. But it is not at all the same thing. And so, whenever I can, I start my journey, not from the great new airports at Vnukovo or Sheremetievo, but from the Kievski Voksal or from one or other of the old Moscow railway stations I have come to know so well. *Voksal*, incidentally, the Russian word for station, derives from our own Vauxhall, evidently the first railway station of which the Russians became aware.

2 *Beyond the Caspian*

To me the most fascinating regions of the Soviet Union have never been European Russia or the Ukraine, but rather, far away to the south and east, the borderlands of Transcaucasia or, further east beyond the Caspian, the legendary cities of Turkestan — Tashkent, Samarkand, and Bokhara — remote and mysterious behind their barrier of deserts and mountains.

And Soviet Central Asia really is remote. From Samarkand recently I travelled up into some mountains, the foothills of the Pamirs. Beyond them lay Afghanistan. A day or two later, after a brief flight eastwards, I found myself in some more mountains, with, on the other side, Chinese Turkestan. Looking out across the flat plain that stretched away to the north, I tried to work out how far I was from the sea. The answer, I decided, was about 2,000 miles to the Arctic Ocean, or, if I turned round and faced the other way, only 1,500 to the Indian Ocean, with the Himalayas and bits of China, India, and Pakistan in between. The distances to the Atlantic and the Pacific seemed hardly worth calculating.

Geographically, the area which is loosely described as Central Asia lies between the Caspian Sea on the west and Lake Baikal to the east. To the north it is bounded by the Arctic Ocean. To the south its limit is roughly set by the greatest system of mountains in the world: the Elburz and Hindu Kush to the west, the Pamirs and Himalayas at the centre, and the Tien Shan and Altai on the eastern flank. The region enclosed by these natural boundaries consists in the main of a vast expanse of arid plain and desert, traversed by two great rivers, the Oxus, or Amu Darya, and the Jaxartes, or Syr Darya, both rising in the great mountain ranges to the south and eventually finding an outlet in the Sea of Aral.

It was along the valleys of these two rivers and their tributaries and also, to some extent, among the foothills of the great mountain ranges, that the civilization, culture and commerce of Central Asia took root and flourished. It was here, too, that the caravans on their way from China to Europe, from the Far East to the Near East, established their staging posts and marketed their wares. And it was thus that in Central Asia there grew up, side by side, two entirely different, but in some respects complementary ways of life: the wandering, half-pastoral, half-military way of life of the nomads, ranging across the steppes on horseback with their flocks and herds, and the sedentary, sophisticated existence of the dwellers in the cities and the oases, which quickly became centres of civilization and of everything, good and bad, that has always gone with it.

The early history of Central Asia is more obscure and harder to disentangle than that of most parts of the world. Nomads kept few records. Reliable sources are few and far between. Fact and fiction, history and legend are inextricably intermingled. Nor is this perhaps surprising. At frequent intervals through the ages marauding hordes of invaders have swept from one quarter or another across the Asian land-mass, slaughtering and destroying as they went. Nations, states, civilizations and religions emerged and then vanished or were absorbed, leaving few clear traces behind them. In the intervals of these dynastic and racial convulsions, remoteness, natural geographical and physical obstacles — the highest mountains and the most formidable deserts in the world — and, no less formidable, the innate suspicion and xenophobia of peoples and rulers, made these areas impossible of access to all but the most resolute travellers.

Not that Central Asia has no history or that its history is without interest. We know that Samarkand was already an important centre of civilization when Alexander of Macedon conquered (and destroyed) it in 329 B.C., while further east Balkh and Merv are two of the oldest inhabited cities in the world, both dating back to the fifth century B.C. or earlier. But there are gaps in our knowledge, which even the most painstaking research has so far failed to fill, and to this day the experts still disagree enthusiastically as to the precise racial origins, provenance and inter-relationship of the various ethnic groups who at one time or another have sprung from, surged through, or settled in this crucible of peoples and nations: Iranians, Turks, Tartars, Turco-Tartars, Huns, Sogdians, Scythians, Sarts, Mongols, Kazaks, Kirghiz, and the rest of them.

The famous inscription at Behistun near Kermanshah dating from the sixth century B.C., which enumerates the satrapies belonging to the Persian Empire of Darius I, includes among them the province of Bactria. This was the region lying between the River Oxus and the mountains of the Paropamisus or Hindu Kush. Indeed not only Bactria, but also the neighbouring regions of Margiana or Merv, Khorezm (later Khiva) and Soghdiana (comprising Samarkand and Bokhara), seem to have been among the conquests of Darius's predecessor Cyrus the Great. And it is probable that the original population of what was later to be known as Turkestan and of the surrounding steppes sprang from the same Iranian stock as their Persian neighbours, and that when Alexander the Great made himself master of Samarkand (or Marakanda, as it was then called), in 329 B.C., the whole area had been part of the Persian Empire for at least two centuries.

Having decisively defeated the Persians under Darius III and made himself master of their country, Alexander spent the next two years consolidating his hold on the area between the Oxus and the Jaxartes, establishing garrisons, pacifying the country round and converting it into a province of his own vastly extended empire, before pushing on across the Hindu Kush in an attempt to conquer India. Meanwhile, in order to protect his newly won dominions from invasion while he was thus engaged, Alexander needed to establish a secure barrier against the fierce nomad races of the north and east. Soon in Bactria a number of new Greek garrison towns were founded; many, including the present Khojend, Herat and Leninabad, bearing the name of Alexandria, while everywhere Greek government and Greek customs superseded the Persian.

After Alexander's death in 323 the Graeco-Bactrian state he had founded seems to have survived for about a century and a half. From Chinese sources we learn of its eventual disruption at the hands of the marauding Tartar tribes who for several centuries to come were to be the masters of Central Asia. But traces of Greek influence and culture did not altogether disappear, and to this day the legend of the great Alexander or 'Iskander' is part of the folk-lore of Central Asia.

It is hard to form any clear idea of the course of events in Central Asia during the thousand years after the death of Alexander the Great, or to unearth more than a series of isolated and often apparently unconnected facts about this period. Once again marauding nomads ranged across the steppes and fought among themselves, and whole provinces changed hands at frequent intervals. In 250 B.C. the Emperor Tsin Chi Hwang-ti of China, determined to defend at any rate his own frontiers against this menace, and in particular against the notorious Hsiung-nu or Huns, began to build the Great Wall of China. Deflected by this formidable barrier, the tide of invaders seems to have swung westward, swamping what remained of Alexander's Graeco-Bactrian kingdom in the foothills of the Hindu Kush.

By the dawn of the Christian era two-and-a-half centuries later the Yue-Chi or Kushans, a branch of the Tung-nu or Eastern Tartars and deadly enemies of the Hsiung-nu or Huns, had become the foremost power in Central Asia and even established formal relations with the Romans. Their vast empire, reaching into Central Asia to the north and India to the south, straddled the mighty range of the Hindu Kush. The Kushans maintained this position of dominance for about 400 years, being finally dislodged around the year 430 of our era by the Ephthalites or White Huns, or, as the Chinese called them, Yetha, a tribe of probably much the same Turco-Mongolian stock as themselves, who formed part of that same wave of invasions and migrations that went sweeping on into Europe under Attila. It is interesting that there are indications of considerable Christian, especially Nestorian, activity in Transoxiana at this time, and we know that in due course a Christian see was established at Samarkand.

Early in the fourth century of our era the Sasanide dynasty had established themselves in Persia, where they were to hold sway, at any rate nominally, for the next four centuries. During this period they maintained an uneasy relationship, sometimes degenerating into open war, with their neighbours on either side, with the Romans of the Eastern Empire on their western frontier and to the east with the White Huns, and later with their successors, the newly emerged Turks.

The Turks proper, or Tu-Kiu, as the Chinese called them, first appear in history around the middle of the sixth century. At this time they were divided into two distinct Khanates. The Eastern Turks controlled a vast region stretching from the Urals to Mongolia, while the Western Turks ruled in Central Asia from the Altai to the Jaxartes. For a time Turks and Persians combined to defeat their common enemies the White Huns and divide up their territories between them — the King of Persia setting his seal on the alliance by marrying the daughter of the Turkish Chief Ruler, or Kakhan. Bactria, so long a thorn in Persia's side, became a Persian province, while the Turks established themselves in Transoxiana. But the alliance did not endure, and soon the Persians were once more involved in three-cornered bickering, with the Turks on the one hand and Byzantium on the other.

Such was the situation in Central Asia, when in the year 632 the Prophet Mohammed, moving from Mecca to Medina, launched from his native Arabia the wave of conquests which, in the space of a few years, brought a great part of the then known world under the sway of Islam. First Palestine and Syria and then, within twenty years of the start of the *Hegira*, the whole of Persia had fallen under Arab rule. Already the Arab armies were reaching out across the Oxus into Turkestan, and the conquest of Transoxiana followed naturally from the overrunning of Sasanian Persia. Between 705 and 715, while other Arab armies marched through Spain on their way to France and established themselves all along the North African coast, the cities of Bactria and Transoxiana fell one after the other to the great Arab conqueror, the Emir Kutaiba-ibn-Muslim, appointed Viceroy of Khorasan in 705, whose armies, in addition to their Arab spearhead, now contained many thousands of locally recruited Persian Moslem auxiliaries. By the year 800 the celebrated Abbasid Caliph Harun al Rashid ruled from his new capital of Bagdad over a vast and prosperous empire stretching from the frontiers of China to the Atlantic coast of Spain.

Within this empire the Persian provinces, now converted to Islam, enjoyed much the same standing as those of Arab population and, having become Moslem, retained a substantial measure of independence. Soon Persia was to all intents and purposes once again an autonomous state under her own rulers, the Samanids, whose dominions embraced the whole of Transoxiana, to which had been given the Arab name of Mawara-al-Nahr, or Mawarannahr, the Land beyond the River. The capital of their dominions was moved at the end of the ninth century from Samarkand to Bokhara.

Having survived until the year 999, the Samanid dynasty was overthrown by the Turkish Karakhanids, who made Samarkand their capital and ruled over most of Transoxiana until the middle of the twelfth century, when they in turn were displaced by the Kara-Kitais, nomads of Chinese culture and probably Mongolian origin, who never embraced Islam.

In Persia and Afghanistan, meanwhile, power had passed to a new tribal group, the Seljuk Turks. From their capital of Merv these now held sway over most of Muslim Asia, including Anatolia, Mesopotamia, Syria, and Palestine. Originally their dominions included Khorezm, today the oasis of Khiva, and the lands along the lower reaches of the Amu-Darya or Oxus. It was not long, however, before there arose in Khorezm an independent line of Turkish Khorezmshahs, former vassals of the Seljuks, who now accepted the suzerainty of neither the Seljuk Sultans nor the Karakitais, whose Empire was already fast disintegrating. Having brought both Samarkand and Bokhara under their own domination, the Khorezmshahs had by the beginning of the thirteenth century made themselves the paramount power in Moslem Central Asia.

3 The Mongols

It was into this tangled world of conflicting and overlapping dynasties and ever-shifting spheres of influence that the breathtaking phenomenon of the Mongol invasions exploded around the year 1220. The Mongols, who had hitherto preferred to call themselves Tartars, were one of a number of nomad tribes who ranged over the rolling country to the north of the Gobi desert and to the south and east of Lake Baikal, in the area which is now Mongolia. The Chinese, as their nearest neighbours, regarded them with mixed feelings, dividing them neatly up into three categories, according to their proximity and their degree of contact with Chinese civilization: the White, the Black and the Savage Mongols. By religion, in so far as they had one, the Mongols were Shamanists or Devil-worshippers — especially the Savage Mongols, who led a roving life in the forests of Transbaikalia, and under the guidance of their tribal shamans or *böge* practised Shamanism in its purest form.

Until the twelfth century the Mongols seem to have made no great impact on the course of history. But in about the year 1155 a son was born to a Mongol chieftain or *khan* named Yesugei Bagatur, who was found to be clutching a clot of dried blood in his tiny hand. The child received at birth the name Temüjin. This he was later to exchange of his own volition for that of Jenghiz Khan, or Ruler of the World.

For the first fifty years and more of his life Jenghiz confined his activities to his own country, first establishing himself as chief of his tribe, and then manœuvring for position with his neighbours. By 1206 he had welded all the tribes of Mongolia into a single confederacy and established himself as its undisputed leader. It was now that he assumed the name of Jenghiz, and the title of Kakhan or Chief Khan. At the same time he reorganized the considerable military forces under his command into units of 10, 100, 1,000 and 10,000 men, the latter, corresponding roughly to a modern division, being known as *tümens*. In these, over and above the natural mobility and manœuvrability of the nomad, he instilled a ruthless discipline based on a clearly established chain of command. Soon he disposed of an

27

extremely formidable military force of a quarter of a million men or more.

According to the Venetian traveller Marco Polo, who was to reach the scene of these events some seventy years later, one of the neighbouring chieftains whom Jenghiz vanquished was the legendary Prester John or Presbyter Johannes, the shadowy Christian priest-king of Central Asia (or, according to other versions, of Abyssinia), 'of whose great empire', says Marco, 'all the world speaks'.

According to Marco, Jenghiz had first sent emissaries to Prester John, asking for his daughter's hand in marriage. This request 'met with a very scornful reception. "Is not Jenghiz Khan ashamed", cried Prester John, "to seek my daughter in marriage? Does he not know that he is my vassal and my thrall? Go back to him and tell him that I would sooner commit my daughter to the flames than give her to him as his wife!"'

When Jenghiz's emissaries returned with this message, 'omitting nothing', Jenghiz flew into a tremendous rage, 'mustered all his followers and got ready the greatest armament that was ever seen or heard of'. With this force, the narrative continues, 'he marched to a wide and pleasant plain called Tenduk which belonged to Prester John, and there encamped. And I assure you that they were such a multitude that their number was beyond count. There he learned to his joy that Prester John was coming; for it was a pleasant plain and a spacious one, where a battle could be fought spaciously.' He had also, we are told, been informed by some wandering Christian soothsayers, whom he consulted and who did a trick with some sticks, that he was going to win the battle. The soothsayers turned out to be right. ('Truthful men', says Marco, 'and true prophets'.) In the spacious battle that ensued Jenghiz was victorious, Prester John was killed, and his descendants became vassals of the Great Khan.

A tribal confederacy of the kind which Jenghiz had formed could only be held together by the prospect of action and booty. Jenghiz now offered to those who followed him the richest prize of all: the conquest of China. A first campaign, undertaken in 1209 against the Tangut state of Hsi-Hsia, proved successful. Jenghiz next turned against Northern China, then ruled over by the Jürchid dynasty. Though the Jürchids were formidable adversaries, superior tactical and strategic skill told in the end. Victory succeeded victory and by 1214 the Mongol armies stood before the walls of Peking. For the time being Jenghiz did not press home his advantage, but temporarily concluded peace. Then, the following year, he resumed hostilities and in 1215 took Peking and all its treasures.

But Jenghiz did not push on into China. Instead, he turned his attention to consolidating his western frontier, sending his general Jebe to occupy the lands of the Karakitai to the west of the Altai Mountains in what is now Kazakstan. This gave the advancing Mongols a common frontier with the powerful Turkish Shahs of Khorezm (or Khiva), who, in addition to Khorezm and Transoxiana, now ruled over most of Afghanistan and Iran, and part of northern India.

It was not long before there was trouble between the neighbours. In 1218 a caravan of several hundred merchants returning from Mongolia to Turkestan were massacred and their goods stolen by the Khorezmian Governor of Otrar. To keep the trade routes open had become an essential principle of Mongol policy. There could be no question of letting the incident pass. But, when Jenghiz sent to protest against the outrage, Mohammed, the Shah of Khorezm, was unwise enough to put his principal envoy to death and to shave off the beards of his two companions.

Jenghiz planned his attack on Khorezm with even greater care and deliberation than his campaign against China. Leaving one of his generals in command of northern China, he himself now assembled a well-equipped army of between 150,000 and 200,000 men and, marching rapidly westwards, reached the River Irtysh in the summer of 1219. The forces of the Shah of Khorezm were more numerous than his, amounting to perhaps 300,000 men. But once again, from the outset, both tactically and strategically, Jenghiz had the upper hand. Striking first at Otrar, he next moved early in 1220 on Bokhara and then on Samarkand, both of which quickly surrendered. At the same time other Mongol armies struck at other parts of the Khorezmshah's domains, capturing city after city. Fleeing through Northern Iran before the advancing Mongols, the Khorezmshah himself eventually took refuge on an island in the Caspian Sea, and there in the year 1220 died miserably of pleurisy.

Having spent the winter of 1220 to 1221 on the Oxus, Jenghiz next attacked Balkh, the capital of Bactria, while his youngest son Tolui raided Khorasan in Persia. In the spring of 1221 he crossed the Hindu Kush and decisively defeated the remaining Khorezmian forces on the Indus. After which, having spent the summer of 1221 in the foothills of the Hindu Kush near Balkh, he once more set out for Mongolia.

Meanwhile the Mongol force of three *tümens* under Jenghiz's generals, Jebe and Sübüdei, who had been sent in pursuit of the Khorezmshah, having successfully overrun north-western Iran and captured Kasvin, established themselves on the Mughan Steppe in what is now Soviet Azerbaijan. They had reached the foothills of the Caucasus. After easily defeating a force of cavalry sent against them by King George IV of Georgia, Jebe and Sübüdei next advanced up the valley of the River Kura as far as Tbilisi, the capital of Georgia, and there defeated the main Georgian army, without, however, taking the city itself. Returning to Persia, they next prepared to invade Russia. Marching once more through Georgia and defeating another Georgian army on the way, they overran the Ukraine and the Crimea, where they spent the winter of 1222–3. That summer they heavily defeated three Russian armies which were sent out to meet them, and then withdrew eastwards, determined to return later in greater strength to complete their task.

Jenghiz himself did not finally reach Mongolia until 1225. On his return to his capital of Karakorum or Black Camp on the Orkhon River, he found that in his absence there had been trouble in China with the Tanguts of Hsi-Hsia. Though now seventy-two years of age and in poor health, he at once re-assembled his forces, and in the spring of 1226 set out to crush the insurgents. It was to be his last campaign. On 24 August 1227 he died; his body was carried back to Mongolia and buried in a grove of trees on the sacred mountain of Burkhan Kaldun.

Jenghiz's death only momentarily checked the Mongol advance. For another fifty years and more the initial impetus was sustained by his sons and grandsons, who made full use of the formidable military machine he had bequeathed to them. 'They made up their mind', says Marco Polo, 'to conquer the whole world.'

Before his death Jenghiz had divided his dominions between his four sons, each tribal region being known as an *ulus*. To Jochi, the eldest, or rather to the latter's son Batu, for Jochi had predeceased his father by a few months, was allotted as his *ulus* the immense area which Jenghiz had conquered west of the River Irtysh, comprising much of what is now Kazakstan and Siberia and reaching as far as the fringes of Russia. This was called the Golden Horde. To his second son, Chaghatai, went most of Turkestan: Transoxiana (or Mawarannahr), Kashgaria, Semirechiye, and Western Jungaria. His third son, Ogetai, on account of his conciliatory character, he appointed his successor as Kakhan. To him he left Eastern Jungaria, Mongolia, and the parts of China now under Mongol rule. His fourth son Tolui inherited the Mongolian homeland, his father's household and treasury, the ancestral pastures, and, most important of all, the seasoned core of shock-troops which constituted the main striking force of the Mongolian armies. In thus distributing his dominions among his heirs, Jenghiz Khan's purpose was not to dismember his empire, but rather to unify it on a basis of family and dynastic co-operation.

In this aim he was not unsuccessful. The next thirty years were to be a period of further Mongol consolidation and expansion. The Mongol hold on Iran and Khorezm was reasserted, Azerbaijan, Armenia and Georgia annexed, Tbīlīsi taken and the Georgian Queen Rusudana driven into the mountains of Imeretia. Korea was invaded and China north of the Yangtze added to the empire. But the most spectacular conquests were those of Batu and his Golden Horde. Between 1237 and 1242, he struck deep into Russia, Poland and Hungary, sweeping all before him and spreading terror throughout Europe. In the winter of 1237 to 1238 Moscow, Vladimir, Rostov, Yaroslavl and Pereyaslavl Zaleski fell to the Mongols. In 1240 Kiev was taken by assault. In March of 1241 the first Mongol *tümen* reached Pesth. In the north one Mongol force defeated the Poles at Chmielnik and then pressed on to Breslau, while another Mongol army overran Lithuania and East Prussia. At Wahlstatt near Liegnitz Archduke Henry of Silesia, with all the chivalry of Poland, Silesia and Moravia, was ambushed and overwhelmed. In a single battle thirty thousand of Henry's troops were killed and his severed head carried in triumph round the walls of Liegnitz. Soon all Hungary had fallen to the Mongols, and the Hungarian King Béla was chased through Croatia into Dalmatia, where he finally took refuge on an island in the Adriatic.

'The Latin world', writes Edward Gibbon, 'was darkened by this cloud of savage hostility: a Russian fugitive carried the alarm to Sweden; and the remote nations of the Baltic and the ocean trembled at the approach of the Tartars, whom their fear and ignorance were inclined to separate from the human species.' And he goes on to record in a characteristic footnote that, fear of the Tartars having stopped the Swedes from fishing as usual for herring off the coast of England, forty or fifty of these fish were sold for a shilling. 'It is', he remarks with true eighteenth-century detachment, 'whimsical enough that the orders of a Mongol Khan, who reigned on the borders of China, should have lowered the price of herrings in the English market.'

Early in 1242, however, just as he was preparing to invade Austria and Bohemia, Batu received the news that his uncle Ogetai, who had undermined his health by excessive drinking and sexual indulgence, was dead. This meant that he himself would have to return to Karakorum to attend the impending Kuriltai, or election of a new Great Khan. And so, reluctantly abandoning his projected campaign, he set out on the long journey home. It can thus be said that Ogetai's death, coming when it did, saved western Europe from a Mongol invasion which could well have reached the Atlantic.

On his eventual return from Karakorum, Batu, apparently abandoning any thought of further conquests, established the capital of the Golden Horde at Sarai on the east bank of the Volga, some sixty miles upstream from Astrakhan. One account of his court beside the Volga comes from Friar John de Plano Carpini, an able elderly Franciscan monk who stopped off there on his way to Karakorum. 'This Bati', writes Friar John, 'holds court right magnificently, for he has doorkeepers and all the other officials like to their Emperor. He sits also in a raised place, as on a throne, with one of his wives … He has tents made of linen. They are large and quite handsome and used to belong to the King of Hungary … In the middle of the dwelling near the door is a table with drink in gold and silver vessels and Bati never drinks without there being singing and guitar-playing. And when he rides out, an umbrella or little awning is always carried over his head. This Bati is kind enough to his own people, but he is greatly feared by them. He is, however, most cruel in war and a most shrewd and crafty warrior, for he has been waging war for a long time.'

Another description of Sarai comes from Friar William of Rubruck, who visited Batu in 1253, also on his way to Karakorum, as an emissary of King Louis IX of France. 'When I saw the *ordu* of Batu', writes Friar William, 'I was astonished, for it seemed like a great city stretched out about his dwelling, with people scattered all about for three or four leagues … Our guide cautioned us to say nothing until Batu should have bid us speak, and then to speak briefly … So we stood there in our robes and barefooted, with uncovered heads, and we were a great spectacle unto ourselves … We stood before him the time to say *Lord have mercy upon me* and all kept profound silence. He was seated on a long seat as broad as a couch, all gilded, and with three steps leading up to it, and a lady was beside him. Men were seated on his right and ladies on his left … A bench with *cosmos* [fermented mare's milk] and big cups of gold and silver, ornamented with precious stones, was in the entry of the tent. He looked at us intently and we at him. And his face was all covered with reddish spots. Finally he bid me speak and our guide told us to bend the knee and speak ... Then he made us sit down and had us given of his milk to drink, and they hold it to be a great honour when anyone drinks *cosmos* with him in his dwelling.'

Henceforward Batu's chief preoccupation was to be with the consolidation of his European conquests west of the Volga. In this he enjoyed the active co-operation of his newly conquered Russian vassals, Jaroslav of Vladimir and his son Alexander Nevski, who, he found, were willing enough to pay tribute to their Mongol overlords in return for being allowed to retain their own religious and cultural identity.

The relationship, even so, was an uneasy one. Friar John Carpini, who met Jaroslav of Vladimir at the court of the new Kakhan, has an interesting story to tell about the manner of his death. 'At this time', he writes, 'Jaroslav, Grand-Duke in a part of Russia called Susdal, died at the Emperor's *orda*. It happens that he was invited by the Emperor's mother to her tent and she gave him to eat and drink with her own hand, as if to honour him. And he went straight back to his lodgings and fell ill and after seven days he was dead and all his body became livid in strange fashion; so that every one believed that he had been poisoned, that they might get free and full possession of his lands.' After this, it appears, the Dowager Empress issued an equally pressing invitation to Jaroslav's son, Alexander Nevski. 'But', says Friar John, 'he would not go, but stayed where he was.'

The succession to Ogetai had not in fact been resolved until 1246, when his son Güyük was elected Kakhan. Güyük was as conscious as his predecessors of the exalted position which he now occupied. John Carpini, who visited him at this time as an emissary of the Pope, took back with him a letter from him to the Pope which is still in the Vatican archives. In this Güyük pointed out to the Pope that all lands from the rising of the sun to its setting were subject to the Great Khan. This, he asserted, could only have come about by God's will. And so he now ordered the Pope to come at the head of all the princes of Europe to do homage to him. 'If', he concluded, 'you do not observe God's command and disobey Our command, We shall know you as Our enemy.' But Güyük died mysteriously in 1248, all Ogetai's male descendants were killed, and in 1251, with Batu's support, a fresh *Kuriltai* bestowed the title of Kakhan on Möngke, the son of Jenghiz's fourth son Tolui.

Power had now passed to a fresh generation of Jenghizkhanids. Though liable to occasional dissensions among themselves, these shared the same compulsive family urge to expand their grandfather's domains still further. The armies that Jenghiz had created were still in existence and the impetus he had given them was still sustained. Sweeping across the uplands of Anatolia, in 1242 the Mongols had defeated the Seljuk Turks at Erzurum and Kayseri, while Batu's advance deep into Hungary had already impressed on the peoples and rulers of Europe the full implications of Mongol power and the need to make contact with this new world-force.

Möngke's reign as Kakhan lasted from 1251 to 1259 and marked in a sense the zenith of the Mongol Empire. Friar William of Rubruck, who after his vist to Batu arrived in Mongolia in 1253, has left a vivid description of Möngke's court and of his own first encounter with the new Kakhan. He and his companions reached Möngke's camp on 3 January 1254, and, having first been searched for hidden arms and sung a short Latin hymn, were admitted to Möngke's presence. 'The house', writes Friar William, 'was all covered inside with cloth of gold and there was a fire burning of briars and wormwood-roots and cattle-dung in a grate in the centre of the dwelling. Möngke was seated on a couch and was dressed in a skin spotted and glossy, like a seal's skin. He is a little man of medium height, aged forty-five years, and a young wife sat beside him.' After some desultory conversation, in the course of which the Mongols, much to Friar William's indignation, debated among themselves whether it would or would not be worth the trouble to conquer his own native land of France, the butlers who were serving Möngke 'gave him so much to drink that he was soon quite drunk', and, the interpreter being also by now quite drunk, the conversation came to an end.

From Möngke Friar William eventually received permission to continue his journey to Karakorum. The Mongol capital, he found, was not as big as the village of St Denis outside Paris. Surrounded by a mud wall with four gates in it, it was divided into a Saracen and a Chinese quarter. In addition to two mosques and twelve temples full of idols, it possessed at least one Christian church, where Friar William attended mass, though he seems to have had grave doubts about the orthodoxy of the local monks. 'I decided to go', he writes, 'though I saw that their sect was full of sorceries and idolatries.' Möngke himself, having first promised to come to church, excused himself at the last moment on the grounds that the bodies of the dead were kept there. That Easter, however, no less than sixty of his subjects were baptized Christians.

Near the city ramparts, enclosed by a high wall, was Möngke's palace, where he held drinking parties twice a year and where his treasure and provisions were stored. Friar William gives a vivid account of its wonders. 'In the entry of this great palace', he writes, 'it being unseemly to bring in there skins of milk and other drinks, Master William the Parisian had made for him a great silver tree, and at its roots are four lions of silver, each with a conduit through it, and all belching forth white milk of mares. And four conduits are led inside the tree to its tops, which are bent downward, and on each of these is also a gilded serpent, whose tail twines round the tree. And from one of these pipes flows wine, from another *caracosmos*, or clarified mares' milk, from another *bal*, a drink made with honey, and from another rice mead, which is called *terracina*; and for each liquor there is a special silver bowl at the foot of the tree to receive it. Between these four conduits in the top, he made an angel holding a trumpet, and underneath the tree he made a vault in which a man can be hid. And pipes go up through the heart of the tree to the angel. In the first place he made bellows, but they did not give enough wind. Outside the palace is a cellar in which the liquors are stored, and there are servants all ready to pour them out when they hear the angel trumpeting. And there are branches of silver on the tree and leaves and fruit. When drink is wanted, the head butler cries to the angel to blow his trumpet. Then he who is concealed in the vault, hearing this, blows the trumpet right loudly. Then the servants who are in the cellar, hearing this, pour the different liquors into the proper conduits, and the conduits lead them down into the bowls prepared for that, and then the butlers draw it and carry it to the palace to the men and women.

'And the palace is like a church, with a middle nave, and two sides, beyond two rows of pillars, and with three doors to the south, and beyond the middle door on the inside stands the tree, and the Khan sits in a high place to the north, so that he can be seen by all; and two rows of steps go up to him: by one he who carries his cup goes up, and by the other he comes down.'

In Karakorum Friar William made friends with a compatriot, William the Parisian, the French craftsman who had made Möngke's silver tree. His name, it transpired, was Buchier, and his brother Roger lived in Paris on the *Grand Pont*. At his house, at a convivial dinner on Palm Sunday, Friar William met his host's wife, who came from Lorraine, and also an Englishman born in Hungary called Basil. William Buchier also made him a special iron to make wafers for Holy Communion, a sculptured image of the Virgin Mary, a silver reliquary, and an unusual belt to take back with him to King Louis, with a precious stone in it which was said to ward off lightning.

During his stay in Karakorum Friar William seems to have had a number of inconclusive discussions with Möngke on the subject of Christianity. During these the Kakhan, as was his wont, refreshed himself at frequent intervals. When Friar William left, he carried back with him a slightly menacing letter from Möngke addressed to King Louis, filled with confused references to his grandfather Jenghiz Khan and concluding with the warning that, should the King of France be unwise enough to attack the Mongols, 'you shall find out what we can do'.

Meanwhile the other members of Möngke's family were already showing what they could do in a number of other directions. In 1253 a major expeditionary force commanded by his brother Hülagü had set out from Mongolia against northern Iran and Mesopotamia. By 1257 Hülagü had captured Alamut, the Eagle's Nest, and most of the other Iranian strongpoints in the Elburz mountains. In 1258 the holy city of Bagdad, the seat of the Caliph, also fell to the Mongols, the Caliph himself being rolled in a carpet and, in order to avoid shedding royal blood, trampled to death. Hülagü thus became the founder of what was to be known as the Il-Khanate of Iran, which, stretching from Kashmir to the Lebanon, with its capital at Tabriz, was to endure for the best part of a century and was marked by a high level of Iranian culture and prosperity. From Hülagü onwards the Il-Khans continued to recognize Mongolian suzerainty, but in practice reigned as independent monarchs.

One of Hülagü's more formidable adversaries in his conquest of Alamut and the surrounding territories was Aladdin, the Sheikh or Old Man of the Mountain, supported by his attendant Assassins. Marco Polo furnishes a wealth of detail on the subject. 'The Sheikh', he tells us, 'held his court with great splendour and magnificence and bore himself most nobly and convinced the simple mountain folk round about that he was a prophet; and they believed it to be the truth.'

But the truth, it appears, was altogether different. In a valley between two mountains the Sheikh had made 'the biggest and most beautiful garden that was ever seen, planted with all the finest fruits in the world and containing the most splendid mansions and palaces that were ever seen, ornamented with gold and with likenesses of all that is beautiful on earth, and also four conduits, one flowing with wine, one with milk, one with honey, and one with water. There were fair ladies there and damsels, and the loveliest in the world, unrivalled at playing every sort of instrument and at singing and dancing. And he gave his men to understand that this garden was Paradise ... At the entrance stood a castle so strong that it need fear no man in the world and there was no other way in except through this castle.'

Into this garden the Sheikh would introduce carefully picked young men from the country round, having first rendered them unconscious with *hashish*, the drug which gave them their name *hashashin*, or assassins, in other words *hashish*-takers. When the young men awoke in the Garden, they were convinced that they were in Paradise, especially as 'the ladies and damsels stayed with them all the time, singing and making music for their delight and ministering to their desires. So these youths had all they could wish for and asked nothing better than to remain there.'

But the Old Man had other plans for them. 'When he wanted emissaries to send on some mission of murder, he would administer the drug to as many as he pleased; and, while they slept, he had them carried into his palace.' When they regained consciousness they were convinced that they had indeed been in Paradise, and their only wish was to return there. The Old Man would then announce that he had the means of sending them back, and would despatch them on some desperate and dangerous mission of assassination: with the result that, 'filled with a great longing to go to this Paradise, they longed for death so that they might go there, and looked forward eagerly to the day of their going'.

In this ingenious manner the Old Man built up a suicide-squad of dedicated killers whose proficiency made him the terror of the whole area. 'Thus it happened', says Marco Polo, 'that no one ever escaped when the Sheikh of the Mountain wanted his death. And I can assure you that many kings and many lords paid tribute to him and cultivated his friendship for fear that he might bring about their death.'

But Hülagü, 'knowing of all the evil deeds this Sheikh was doing, made up his mind that he should be crushed', and besieged him in his castle of Alamut for three years and in the end captured and killed him. 'And from that time', says Marco Polo a trifle smugly, 'there have been no more of these Sheikhs and no more Assassins.'

But here he was wrong. After their defeat by Hülagü, the Ismailis, as the Old Man's sect now called themselves, simply went underground, electing their leaders in secret and continuing, when the need arose, to carry out well-planned and well-executed murders. Even King Edward I of England, the so-called Hammer of the Scots, narrowly escaped assassination at their hands — or so it was said. With the passage of a few centuries, however, the activities of the Ismailis became more respectable, their leader eventually moving by way of India to England, where during the present century the Aga Khan, leader of the Ismaili sect and direct descendant of the Old Man of the Mountain, achieved, presumably without recourse to any nefarious practices, the Triple Crown of the British Turf.

4 *In Xanadu did Kubla Khan...*

While Hülagü was busy conquering Persia and Mesopotamia, his brother Kublai had turned his attention to Southern China, and there achieved such successes that in the end he aroused the jealousy of their elder brother Möngke, the Kakhan, who in 1257 deprived him of the command of the expeditionary force and took it over himself. But in 1259 Möngke died in his camp in Szechwan – of dysentery, it was said – and was carried back in state to his family's burial place in the Altai mountains. 'And here', observes Marco Polo, never at a loss for useful information, 'is a remarkable fact: when the body of a Great Khan is being carried to this mountain – be it forty days' journey or more or less – all those who are encountered along the route by which the body is being conveyed are put to the sword by the attendants who are escorting it. "Go!" they cry, "and serve your lord in the next world." For they truly believe that all those whom they put to death must go and serve the Khan in the next world. And they do the same thing with horses: when the Khan dies, they kill all his best horses, so that he may have them in the next world. It is a fact that, when Mongu Khan died, more than 20,000 men were put to death, having encountered his body on the way to the burial.'

With Möngke dead and buried and sent thus well escorted to the next world, it only remained for Kublai to quell the opposition of yet another brother (who also happened to die). After this he himself assumed the title of Kakhan, and was soon in control of the greater part of Möngke's empire, over which he reigned successfully for the next thirty-five years, becoming, with the extinction of the Sung Dynasty in 1279, the first foreigner (or, as the Chinese put it, 'barbarian') to rule over the whole of China. From this new forward base Kublai was to launch a number of ambitious but unrewarding military expeditions against Japan and the countries of South-East Asia, where the Mongols, invincible in the open plain, quickly became bogged down in the steamy heat of the tropical jungle.

China had been the scene of Kublai's greatest victories and from now on he spent most of his time there, falling more and more into the ways and traditions of his own Chinese subjects. In 1264 he moved the capital of his empire from Karakorum to Peking, or, as it was now called, Khan-Balik, and in 1271 assumed on behalf of his dynasty the Chinese name of Yuan. He also took care that his heirs should enjoy the full benefits of Chinese culture and education.

It was during Kublai's reign, in the year 1265, that two Venetian brothers, Maffeo and Niccolò Polo, arrived in China. They had started by travelling as far as Constantinople, and thence to the Crimea on a trading mission to the Tartars. From the Crimea they made their way, first to the capital of the Golden Horde at Sarai on the Volga, and then after various adventures to Bokhara. There they fell in with 'an envoy from Hülagü, the Lord of the Levant, on his way to the Great Khan of all the Tartars, who ... lived at the ends of the earth in an east-north-easterly direction'. On learning that they were from the west and were merchants, this personage addressed them as follows: 'Sirs, if you will trust me, I can offer you an opportunity of great profit and great honour ... I assure you that the Great Khan of the Tartars has never seen any Latin and is exceedingly desirous to meet one. Therefore, if you will accompany me to him, I assure you that he will be very glad to see you and will treat you with great honour and great bounty.'

And so it turned out. Setting forth with the Tartar envoy, Maffeo and Niccolò travelled for a whole year along the old Silk Road, passing through the great deserts to the north of Tibet and finally arriving safe and sound at the court of the Great Khan, where Kublai seems to have been as pleased to see them as Hülagü's envoy had said he would be. He welcomed them, we are told, with lavish hospitality and plied them with endless questions about the Emperor and the Pope and the practices of the Roman Church and the customs of the Latins, and the Kings, Princes and Governments of Europe. 'And Messer Niccolò and Messer Maffeo told him all the truth about each matter in due order, well and wisely, like the wise men they were.' With the result that, 'when the Great Khan ... had heard all about the Latins ... he was exceedingly pleased and made up his mind to send emissaries to the Pope and asked the two brothers to go on this mission with one of his barons'.

The purport of this somewhat surprising mission was twofold. First, the Pope was to be asked to send 'up to a hundred men learned in the Christian religion, well versed in the seven arts, and skilled to argue and demonstrate to idolaters and those of other persuasions that their religion is utterly mistaken ... men able to show by clear reasoning that the Christian religion is better than theirs'. And secondly, the Polos were to 'bring oil from the lamp that burns above the sepulchre of God in Jerusalem'.

In spite of a special tablet of gold, given them by Kublai, 'on which it was written that ... wherever they went they should be given all the lodging they might need and horses and men to escort them from one land to another', it took the brothers three years to reach Acre in Palestine, and when they finally arrived there they were told by the Papal Legate that the Pope, Clement IV, had died. They accordingly went on to Venice, where they arrived in 1269 and where Niccolò found that in his absence his wife had died and his little son Marco had become a youth of fifteen.

In Venice they waited for two more years for a new Pope to be chosen. But now their luck was in. Their friend the Papal Legate, whom they had met in Acre and who had become interested in their mission, was now elected Pope as Gregory X, and in 1271 they set out on their return journey with every encouragement from the Supreme Pontiff, who gave them his blessing and sent with them not only letters for Kublai Khan and gifts and oil from the Holy Sepulchre, but two Dominican friars with 'plenary authority to ordain priests and bishops and grant absolution as fully as he could himself'. With them, in addition to the friars, went Niccolò's young son Marco.

The Polos' return journey was full of incident. They had got no further than Armenia when 'Bundukdari the Sultan of Egypt, came into Armenia with a great host and wrought great havoc in the country, and the emissaries went in peril of their lives'. Unfortunately for the prospects of Christianity in Kublai's empire, this was too much for the Dominicans. 'When the friars saw this,' writes Marco, 'they were scared at the prospect of going further and eventually declared they would not go on.' And so the three Polos went on by themselves.

The rest of their journey to the court of the Great Khan took them three-and-a-half more years, and by the time they arrived the boy Marco was twenty-one. Once again Kublai was glad to see them and entertained them lavishly, 'making them welcome with mirth and merry-making'. He was pleased, too, by the letters from the Pope, and delighted with the holy oil. When he saw young Marco, he at once asked who he was. 'Sire,' replied Niccolò, 'he is my son and your liege man.'

'He is heartily welcome,' said the Khan politely.

Thus began the remarkable career of Marco Polo, *Il Milione*, as his contemporaries laughingly called him. 'Observing his wisdom', we are told, Kublai Khan now took him into his service, entrusting him with a series of important missions, all of which he fulfilled with a shrewdness and judgment far beyond his years. Marco was to remain in Kublai's service for the next seventeen years. He possessed remarkable powers of observation, and, failing this, of imagination. 'Messer Marco', he tells us, 'observed more of the peculiarities of this part of the world than any other man, because he travelled more widely in these outlandish regions than any man who was ever born and because he gave his mind more intently to observing them.' And indeed, after reading his account of his experiences, it is hard to dissent from this somewhat self-satisfied judgment.

To Marco we owe a fascinating account of Kublai and his court. 'Kublai', he writes, 'is a man of good stature, neither short nor tall, but of moderate height. His limbs are well fleshed out and modelled in due proportion. His complexion is fair and ruddy like a rose, the eyes black and handsome, the nose shapely and set squarely in place.' And he goes on to tell of the Great Khan's four lawful wives and also of his numerous concubines. These were selected for him every two years or so by special emissaries, 'according to the standard of beauty which he lays down for them ... inspecting and surveying every girl, point by point, to see whether they are well formed and in harmony', and awarding them marks in accordance with a carefully laid down scale, before passing them on to the barons' wives, 'who are instructed to observe them carefully at night in their chambers, to make sure that they are virgins and not blemished or defective in any member, that they sleep sweetly without snoring, and that their breath is sweet and they give off no unpleasant odour. Then those who are approved are divided into groups of six, who serve the Khan for three days and three nights at a time in his chamber and his bed, ministering to all his needs. And he uses them according to his pleasure. After three days and three nights, in come the next six damsels. And so they continue in rotation throughout the year.'

Kublai was accustomed to spend December, January and February in Khan-Balik, or Peking, the capital city of Cathay. His palace, 'the largest that ever was seen', stood approximately on the site of the existing Forbidden City, surrounded on four sides by a wall, each side being one mile long. 'Within this wall is another wall ... and within this wall is the Khan's palace. The Palace itself has a very high roof. Inside the walls of the halls and chambers are all covered with gold and silver and decorated with pictures of dragons and birds and horsemen and various breeds of beasts and scenes of battle. The ceiling is similarly adorned, so that there is nothing to be seen anywhere but gold and pictures. The hall is so vast and so wide that a meal might well be served there for more than 6,000 men' — the same number, it may be observed, that can today sit down to dinner in Mao Tse Tung's Great Hall of the People only a few hundred yards away.

At these court banquets, the Great Khan himself sat 'at the northern end of the hall, so that he faced south', with his principal wife next to him on the left, to his right on a lower level his sons in order of age, and the rest of the company also arranged to a strict order of precedence, with barons waiting at table, wearing napkins over their mouths and noses, and a band that struck up every time the Great Khan was about to drink. And Marco describes 'the great lion' that was led on such occasions into the Great Khan's presence, 'and, as soon as it sees him, it flings itself down prostrate before him with every appearance of deep humility and seems to acknowledge him as lord. There it stays without a chain, and is indeed a thing to marvel at.

'Between the inner and the outer walls, of which I have told you, are stretches of park land with stately trees. The grass grows here in abundance, because all the paths are paved and built up fully two cubits above the level of the ground, so that no mud forms on them and no rainwater collects in puddles, but the moisture trickles over the lawns, enriching the soil and promoting a lush growth of herbage. In these parks there is a great variety of game, such as white harts, musk-deer, roebuck, stags, squirrels, and many other beautiful animals.'

We also learn of 'the mound fully 100 yards in height and over a mile in circumference ... thickly covered with trees and evergreens', which the Khan had had made outside the walls on the northern side of the palace and which today is known as Coal Hill; and of the new city of Taidu which he had built across the river from Khan-Balik to house the less reliable citizens of the old capital; and of the 20,000 prostitutes who lived in the suburbs, 'serving the needs of men for money', with their own Captain-General and subordinate Captains. 'This is because, whenever ambassadors come to the Great Khan on his business and are maintained at his expense, which is done on a lavish scale, the captain is called upon to provide one of these women every night for the ambassador and one for each of his attendants. They are changed every night and receive no payment; for this is the tax they pay to the Great Khan.'

Marco describes in great detail the different kinds of hunting which Kublai engaged in: with thousands of leopards and lynxes and hounds, all trained in the chase, and 'lions of immense size, bigger than those of Egypt, with handsome, richly coloured fur with stripes lengthwise, of black, orange and white ... trained to hunt wild boars and bulls, bears, wild apes, stags, roebuck and other game'. 'A grand sight it is', adds Marco, 'to see the stately creatures that fall a prey to these lions. He also has', he continues, 'a great many eagles trained to take wolves and foxes and fallow deer and roedeer ... Those that are trained to take wolves are of immense size and power, for there is never a wolf so big that he escapes capture by one of these eagles. The great Khan always rides on the back of four elephants, in a very handsome shelter of wood, covered inside with cloth of beaten gold and outside with lion skins. Here he always keeps twelve gerfalcons of the best he possesses and is attended by several barons to entertain him and keep him company. When he is travelling in this shelter on the elephants, and other barons who are riding in his train call out, "Sire, there are cranes passing," and he orders the roof of the shelter to be thrown open and so sees the cranes, he bids his attendants fetch such gerfalcons as he may choose and lets them fly. And often the gerfalcons take the cranes in full view while the Great Khan remains all the while on his couch. And this affords him great sport and recreation.'

Marco was also impressed by Kublai's paper currency. 'You might as well say he has mastered the art of alchemy ... sheets of paper ... cut up into rectangles of various sizes, longer than they are broad ... With these pieces of paper they can buy anything and pay for anything ... none dares refuse it on pain of losing his life.' By his use of coal, 'a sort of black stone, which is dug out of veins in the hillsides and burns like logs ... if you put them on the fire in the evening ... they will continue to burn all night.' By his charity to the poor — 'not a day passes but twenty or thirty thousand bowls of rice, millet and panic are doled out and given away'. By his system of post-roads, with posting-stations and runners and post-horses at intervals of twenty-five or thirty miles, by which messengers managed to cover 250 or 300 miles a day with news for the Great Khan. ('The whole organization is so stupendous and so costly that it baffles speech and writing.') By the efficiency of his Imperial General Staff: 'twelve great and powerful barons to supervise all decisions concerning the movement of the armies, changes in the high command and dispatch of troops to one theatre or another ... it also rests with them to sort out the staunch and fearless fighters from the fainthearted, promoting the former and degrading those who prove incompetent or cowardly.' And, last but not least, by his five thousand astrologers and soothsayers of all denominations, 'Christian, Saracen, and Cathayan ... If anyone proposes to embark on some important enterprise ... he will consult the astrologers ... and those who prove to be the most accurate in their predictions, will be reckoned the most accomplished masters of their art.'

In 1292, just twenty years after they had left Venice, Marco and his father and uncle were given permission to leave Khan-Balik, being charged with the task of escorting the Princess Kokachim, a young lady of seventeen 'of great beauty and charm', whom Kublai was sending, accompanied by three lords, to be the bride of his nephew Hülagü's son, the Il-Khan Argun. 'The Great Khan, who was very fond of the three, granted this favour with some reluctance and gave leave to the three Latins to travel with the three lords and the lady.' Before setting out, the Polos 'took grateful leave of the Great Khan', who presented them with four heavy gold tablets, to serve as passports on their journey.

By the time the travellers reached their destination King Argun, unfortunately, had died from drinking what he mistakenly believed to be the Elixir of Life. But instead the Princess Kokachim married his son Ghazan, and the Polos then continued on their way, taking ship from Trebizond to Constantinople and thence back to Venice, where they arrived early in 1295, just twenty-three years after they had started. Kokachim, we learn, was sad to see her travelling companions depart and 'wept for grief at their going'.

The welcome the travellers received on their return to their native city was anything but enthusiastic. Having long believed them to be dead, their families failed to recognize them and viewed with disfavour these strange creatures 'with a touch of the Tartar about them' who claimed to be related to them. Their clothes, too, worn, shabby, and very, very dirty, aroused universal repugnance.

But the story has a happy ending. At a great banquet which they somehow managed to attend the Polos suddenly ripped open the seams of their obnoxious garments and let fall from them whole showers of the rubies, diamonds and emeralds they had brought back with them. Which, life being what it is, immediately convinced all concerned of the authenticity of their claims.

From Marco Polo's journeys and experiences and from the information he collected from one source or another while in the service of the Great Khan came to be written perhaps the most famous of all traveller's tales. Three years after his return, in the year 1298, Marco had the misfortune to be taken prisoner by the Genoese in a battle between Venetian and Genoese ships off the island of Korčula in the Adriatic, which proudly claims him as a native and where a house said to be his is still shown to admiring visitors. During the next three years, which he spent in jail in Genoa, he compiled, with the help of a fellow prisoner with literary leanings, named Rustichello, an account of his wanderings and of the countries he had visited, entitled *Divisament dou Monde, A Description of the World*, which can be read with as much pleasure today as when it was written, and from which it is possible to piece together a vivid and immediate, though perhaps not always entirely accurate, picture of Kublai Khan and his world.

By moving his capital to Peking, Kublai had to some extent lost touch with Karakorum and the Western Khanates. Already in Central Asia and in Mongolia itself his authority was being challenged by Qaydu, a grandson of Ogetai, and it can be said that in his reign began the disintegration of the empire which Jenghiz Khan had founded, or at any rate its transformation into a kind of loose confederation.

Though Kublai's immediate successor duly defeated Qaydu and re-asserted his supremacy over the Western Khanates, during the sixty years that followed the feebleness of successive Yuan emperors and their remoteness from the centre of power gradually weakened their control and undermined the coherence of their dominions. With the opening of the oceanic trade routes, the transcontinental caravan trade, which had once played such an important part in unifying the Mongol Empire, began to decline. During the first half of the fourteenth century the links which connected the different Khanates with each other and with Peking gradually grew weaker, and by the time the founder of the Chinese Ming Dynasty finally swept away the last of the Mongol Yuans in 1369, the empire they had once ruled over had in fact ceased to exist.

Henceforward, under the Mings (1368–1644) and their successors the Manchus (1644–1911), Mongolia itself came to be little more than a province of China under princes who paid tribute to Peking. But more important still in its impact on the Mongols, more important even than the eventual approach of Russia from the west, was to be the gradual spread throughout Mongolia from the end of the sixteenth century onwards of Lamaist Buddhism from Tibet, which in time was completely to transform the nature and character of the Mongol people.

While Kublai and his successors fell more and more into Chinese ways and so lost touch with the remainder of their empire, the Western Khanates also shed many of their original Mongol characteristics. And with time they, too, not unnaturally came to attach ever less importance to the tenuous links which in theory still bound them to Peking.

Batu had died in 1255. His brother Berke, having disposed, one after the other, of Batu's sons, succeeded him as Khan of the Golden Horde in 1258. He was the first Mongol ruler to embrace Islam. This soon became the dominant religion of the Horde, while the Tartar language was accepted as its *lingua franca*. During the next hundred years or so the rulers of the Golden Horde were engaged in constant hostilities and disputes with their neighbours and kinsmen the Il-Khans of Persia over the possession of Transcaucasia and the Caucasus, which Möngke, when Kakhan, had taken away from the Golden Horde in order to give them to his brother Hülagü.

In Turkestan, too, there was confusion. After the death in 1241 of Jenghiz's second son, Chaghatai, his descendants continued to reign for the best part of a century in the *ulus* which his father had allotted to him and which, it will be recalled, comprised most of Turkestan. The history of the Chaghatai Khans is obscure, and there is no reason to suppose that any of them were at all remarkable. They seem to have retained their nomadic traditions longer than their kinsmen, and under their rule the towns and cities of the oases fell into decay. Indeed one of them, Burag Khan, in order to keep his hand in, is reported to have actually plundered and sacked his own cities of Bokhara and Samarkand before setting out on a campaign. Like the rulers of the Golden Horde, the Chaghatai Khans became Mohammedans in the second half of the thirteenth century, and were likewise engaged in almost constant hostilities with the Il-Khans. They were also plagued by constant internal dissensions. By the middle of the fourteenth century these had degenerated into complete and prolonged anarchy, in the course of which the Chagatai *ulus* appears to have more or less disintegrated.

5 Timur-i-Lenk

This period of general confusion ended abruptly with the emergence in the 1360s of another great conqueror: Timur or Tamerlane. 'His birth', writes Gibbon, 'was cast on one of those periods of anarchy which announce the fall of the Asiatic dynasties, and open a new field to adventurous ambition.'

Timur was born in 1336 at Kesh in Mawarannahr near Shahr-i-Sabz, not many miles to the south of Samarkand. He was the son of a chieftain of the Barlas clan, Turkish or possibly Mongolian by race, and a devout Mohammedan. Though an outstanding chess player and great patron of the arts, he never learned to read or write. Literally interpreted, Timur signifies 'man of iron', and the longer form, Tamburlaine or Tamerlane, is derived from Timur-i-Lenk, Timur the Lame, as he was called after a wound he received in battle had lamed him for life. While still a youth, Timur made himself a name as a partisan leader. Soon he had achieved a position of ascendancy among the tribes of Mawarannahr and had put himself at the head of a considerable military force. By 1370 he had become the undisputed ruler of Mawarannahr and had made Samarkand his capital. Modelling himself on Jenghiz Khan, he now set out to conquer the world,

After spending the ten years from 1370 to 1380 in consolidating his position in Mawarannahr and dealing with his immediate neighbours in Kashgaria and Khorezm, Timur invaded Khorasan. Defeating the Il-Khans, he was soon master of the whole of Persia, pushing up northwards into Azerbaijan and Georgia and driving southwards to sack Isfahan and Shiraz. For a time he allied himself with Toktamish, the Khan of the Golden Horde. But it soon became clear that Toktamish was a threat to the borders of his empire, and by 1385 the erstwhile allies were bitter rivals, fighting each other for the Caucasus and Transcaucasia and raiding each other's territory. Timur won a first victory over Toktamish at Kunduzha, east of the Volga near Samara, and in 1392 resumed his campaigns in Persia, driving on through Fars into Mesopotamia, Anatolia and Georgia. But the power of the Golden Horde had remained unbroken and, in 1395,

48

The Mountains of Heaven

The Pool of Hodja Akhror

Medresseh of Abdul Aziz Khan ▷

Shakh Zindeh, Samarkand

Shakh Zindeh

Urgut: The Sacred Pool

Bokhara: at prayer

Bokhara: husband and wife

In the Chai Khana

Bokhara: in the Bazaar

Bokhara: in the Ark

Bokhara: in the Bazaar

Penjikent: the foothills of the Pamirs ▷

Mongolia: a Mongol and his horse

Mongolia: Gandang Monastery,
the Chief Lama and his Chaplain

Mongolia: horsemen

massing his forces, Timur again turned against Toktamish, striking up into Transcaucasia from Azerbaijan and finally crushing him decisively in April in a battle at Tatartub on the banks of the River Terek, which he himself always regarded as the most important of all his victories. After this he swept on across the Kuban Steppe and utterly destroyed the Golden Horde's capital at Sarai on the Volga, before returning for a while to Samarkand. Crossing the Hindu Kush and the Indus, Timur next invaded northern India, and in 1398, 'marching with such vigour that he overtook the birds', stormed and sacked Delhi and Meerut.

He was now sixty-two. After returning briefly to Samarkand in May 1399, he moved later that year to his favourite winter quarters in Karabagh in the Eastern Caucasus. Once again there had been trouble with the Georgians, and in the autumn Timur decided to wipe them out. The first snows had already fallen, but the Tartars pushed on into the mountains, felling the forests as they advanced. Everything along the line of their advance they destroyed. Everywhere the towns and villages were put to the sack and all Christian churches razed to the ground. Especial care was taken to uproot the vines, for it was well known how much the Georgians depended on the wine they made from them. But the Georgians under their king, George VII, fought back fiercely; the winter of 1399 to 1400 was exceptionally severe; and Timur's troops suffered serious losses. In the end he decided to suspend hostilities until the spring, and returned to Karabagh to celebrate the birth of his latest great-grandson. After some months of lavish feasting at the expense of his ally the King of Shirvan, Timur gave orders for a fresh campaign against the Georgians, the fifth. This time the Georgians quickly took to the hills, leaping out at the Tartars from their caverns and hiding-places in the mountain-sides. But Timur had archers lowered in baskets from above, who shot oil-steeped fire-arrows into the caves and smoked them out. In the end Tbilisi was taken; from the steeples of its churches the muezzin called the faithful to prayer; many feudal lords made their submission and became Moslems, and those who did not were for the most part beheaded. King George himself escaped into the Western Caucasus, whence he reopened negotiations and eventually came to terms with Timur, agreeing to pay a heavy tribute and recognize him as his suzerain.

In 1401 Timur, setting out once more from Karabagh, stormed Bagdad and Damascus and broke the power of the Mamelukes in Syria. Then he turned his attention to the Ottoman Turks, already well on their way to becoming a world power. Six years earlier in 1396, the Ottoman Sultan, Bayazid the Thunderbolt, had utterly defeated the Last Crusade at Nicopolis on the Danube. Now, while on the one hand threatening Constantinople, he was at the same time pushing deep into eastern Anatolia and beginning to encroach on Timur's own preserves in Armenia. Timur warned him not to go too far. An ant, he said abrasively, should not go to war with an elephant. The tone of Bayazid's reply was also far from conciliatory. 'O ravening dog named Timur', it began.

The direct clash did not come until the summer of 1402. By then Timur was ready. Advancing westwards right into Anatolia, he encountered Bayazid at Ankara, utterly defeated him, and, taking him prisoner, carried him off in a cage—or so it was said. After which he went on to sack the city of Brusa, and in December the Christian stronghold of Ismir or Smyrna.

By the end of 1402 Timur was master of all western Asia from the Aegean to Turkestan. He now set out once more for Samarkand, this time in order to prepare for the invasion of China, which at the beginning of the fifteenth century was the richest country on earth.

Although, like Jenghiz, a leader of nomad armies, Timur also enjoyed the luxuries of city life. Under him Samarkand had become a centre of civilization, and one of the most beautiful cities of its age. To Don Ruy Gonzalez de Clavijo, who arrived there in September 1404 as Ambassador of Henry III of Castile to Tamerlane, we owe a fascinating first-hand account of Samarkand during what were to be the last months of Tamerlane's reign. The occasion, indirectly, of Clavijo's embassy had been Tamerlane's victory over Bayazid at Ankara. Timur's defeat of the Turks at Ankara had had the effect of deflecting them from Constantinople and so keeping Byzantium out of the clutches of the infidel for another half-century. And this, not unnaturally, had made him an object of greater interest than ever to the princes of Europe, whose own efforts against the Turks had been considerably less successful.

Already in the spring of 1402, Henry III, anxious for news, had sent to the Levant two envoys who found Tamerlane encamped outside Ankara. And Tamerlane, having graciously received them, had in his turn sent an embassy to Spain with many rich gifts for King Henry. These, in addition to a profusion of jewels, included two Christian maidens hand-picked from Bayazid's seraglio and answering to the names of Maria and Angelina, whom he now 'sent back for safe keeping'. It was as a return for this embassy that in May 1403 King Henry despatched Clavijo, who was one of his Chamberlains, together with a friar named Alfonso Paez, and Gomez de Salazar, an officer of the Royal Guard. They were accompanied on their journey by Tamerlane's own envoy to King Henry, now on his way home.

Clavijo and his companions had hoped to come up with Tamerlane in Eastern Georgia, in the plains of Karabagh, near the lower reaches of the Araxes, where they had heard that he proposed to spend the winter. But they were delayed by inclement weather and so were obliged to follow on to Samarkand.

From Cadiz the journey to Samarkand took fifteen months. First by ship to Constantinople and on to Trebizond (the seat at this time of another Christian Emperor, who had lately become a vassal of Tamerlane). Then by land for another three thousand miles through eastern Turkey and northern Persia to Balkh and across the Oxus by way of Termez and Shahr-i-Sabz to Samarkand.

By the last day of August 1404 the travellers had reached the vicinity of Samarkand. They were now conducted to an orchard, enclosed within a high wall and laid out with ornamental avenues and plantations of fruit trees and streams of running water, with pheasants and different kinds of deer roaming at large among them. In this orchard were a number of palaces, handsomely decorated with tiles of blue and gold and other colours, where they rested for a week, during which Tamerlane sent them some sheep and a number of horses, some to eat and some to ride, as well as handsome robes of gold brocade. Finally on the morning of 8 September they were escorted across the plain to the city of Samarkand, to be received in audience by Tamerlane in one of his palaces on the outskirts of the city. With them went Tamerlane's Ambassador to King Henry III. 'Of our company', Clavijo tells us, 'was that Tartar envoy, whom Timur had sent to the King of Castile, but at his present appearance his friends laughed much, for he was dressed by us in the manner and fashion of a gentleman of Spain.'

'Samarkand', writes Clavijo of Tamerlane's capital, 'stands in a plain and is surrounded by a rampart or wall of earth with a very deep ditch ... The city itself is rather larger than Seville, but lying outside Samarkand are great numbers of houses which form extensive suburbs ... All round the City are orchards and vineyards, spreading for a league or two into the surrounding country. In between are streets and open squares, all densely populated and here all kinds of goods are on sale. Thus it is that the population outwith the City is more numerous than the population within the walls. Among the orchards outwith Samarkand are the most noble and beautiful houses and here Timur has his many palaces and pleasure grounds. Round and about the great men of the government also here have their estates and country houses, each standing within its orchard: and so numerous are these gardens and vineyards surrounding Samarkand that a traveller who approaches the city sees only a great mountainous height of trees and the houses embowered among them remain invisible. Through the streets of Samarkand, as through its gardens outside and inside, pass many water-conduits, and in these gardens are the melon-beds and cotton-growing lands.

'The melons of this countryside are abundant and very good, and at the season of Christmas there are so many melons and grapes to be had that it is indeed marvellous. Every day camels bring in their loads of melons from the country and it is a wonder how many are sold and eaten in the market ... Beyond the suburbs of Samarkand stretch the great plains where are situated many hamlets, these being all well populated, for here the immigrants are settled, whom Timur has caused to be brought hither from all the foreign lands that he has conquered. The soil of the whole province of Samarkand is most fertile, producing great crops of wheat. There are abundant fruit-trees also with rich vineyards: the livestock are magnificent, beasts and poultry all of a fine breed ... The richness and abundance of this great capital and the surrounding district are a wonder to behold.'

And Clavijo goes on to enumerate the trades encouraged by Timur 'in order to make his capital the noblest of cities', and the master-craftsmen of all the nations carried off by him from the cities he had conquered: weavers from Damascus, bowmakers and armourers, gunsmiths from Turkey, silversmiths and masons, engineers and bombardiers. Also 'the merchandise imported from distant and foreign countries': leather and linens from Russia and Tartary; silk from Cathay, the finest silk in the world, and musk and rubies; from India, 'the lesser spiceries, such as nutmeg and cloves and mace with cinnamon'; and the cooked meats and bread and fruit—'all these viands and victuals set out in a decent and cleanly manner in the squares and open spaces of the town'. Last of all, he describes the Castle, 'not built on a height, but protected on all sides by deep ravines ... making it impregnable'. Here Tamerlane kept his treasures and here a thousand armourers were kept at work unceasingly making bows and arrows and armour and helmets.

In the Royal Palace the envoys were passed on from one group of court officials to another until they finally reached the imperial presence. 'We found Timur', writes Clavijo, 'seated under what might be called a portal, which was before the entrance of a most beautiful palace that appeared in the background. He was sitting on the ground, but upon a raised dais before which there was a fountain that threw up a column of water into the air backwards, and in the basin of the fountain were floating red apples. His Highness had taken his place on what appeared to be small mattresses stuffed thick and covered with embroidered silk cloth, and he was leaning on his elbow against some round cushions that were heaped up behind him. He was dressed in a cloak of plain silk without any embroidery, and he wore on his head a tall white hat on the crown of which was displayed a *balas* ruby, the same being further ornamented with pearls and precious stones. As soon as we came in sight of his Highness, we made him our reverence, bowing and putting the right knee to the ground and crossing our arms over the breast. Then we advanced a step and again bowed, and a third time we did the same, but on this occasion kneeling on the ground and remaining in that posture ... His Highness, however, commanded us to arise and stand close up to him that he might the better see us, for his sight was no longer good, indeed, he was so infirm and old that his eyelids were falling over his eyes, and he could barely raise them to see ... Timur now enquired of us for the health of the King our Master saying: "How is it with my son your King? How goes it with him? Is his health good?" We suitably answered and then proceeded to set out the message of our embassy at length, his Highness listening carefully to all that we had to say.'

Later the audience took an interesting and significant turn. Clavijo had been seated by error in an inferior position to the envoy of the Ming Emperor of Cathay, who, it seemed, had been sent by his master to demand tribute of Tamerlane. But this Tamerlane at once put right, sending one of his lords in waiting 'to inform this Chinaman that the ambassadors of the King of Spain, the good friend of Timur and his son, must indeed take place above him who was the envoy of a robber and a bad man, the enemy of Timur, and that he his envoy must sit below us: and if only God were willing, he Timur would before long see to and dispose matters so that never again would any Chinaman dare come with such an embassy as this man had brought'. Or, according to another version, that of the German captive Schiltberger, Tamerlane 'sent him to tell his Lord that he would neither pay tribute nor be subject to him, and that he should himself pay *him* a visit'. 'This Emperor of China', adds Clavijo, 'is called Chays Khan or Emperor of the Nine Empires, but the Tartars call him Tanguz, a name given in mockery, signifying Pig Emperor.'*

After the formal audience there followed a banquet at which immense quantities of roast horse-meat and mutton were served on dishes of gold, silver and porcelain, followed by melons and peaches and grapes, and gold and silver goblets of mare's milk sweeted with sugar. Then came the display of the presents brought to Tamerlane by Clavijo, together with some presents sent by the Sultan of Egypt, after which Clavijo and his companions were escorted by the Chief Doorkeeper back to their lodgings 'in a house standing in a well-watered orchard' near Tamerlane's own palace.

Clavijo next describes Tamerlane's various residences in and around Samarkand. The palace in which Tamerlane had granted them their first audience, with silken tents pitched in its gardens, was known as Dilkusha or Heartsease. On the following Friday he removed to another garden 'where was also a very sumptuous palace ... still being built and known as *Bagh i Chinar*, The Garden of the Plane Trees'. Three days later he moved on to yet another 'place of great beauty, with before its entrance gate a high portal, very finely built of brick ornamented with tiles wrought variously in gold and blue ... throughout the garden many tents had been pitched with pavilions of coloured tapestries for shade, and the silk hangings were of diverse patterns, some being strangely embroidered and others plain in design ... The interior was all most richly furnished with hangings on the walls and within there was a chamber with three arched alcoves which were sleeping places, each with a raised dais, the walls and flooring being decorated with coloured tiles ... The largest of the three alcoves was the one facing you and here stood a screen made of silver and gilt ... In front of this screen was a bed made up from mattresses, some covered with cloth of gold and some with silk worked with gold thread. One mattress was placed above the other on the floor and this was His Highness's couch. The walls were covered with rose coloured silk hangings, ornamented with silver-gilt spangles, each set with an emerald or pearl or other precious stone. Above these hung strips of silk, to which were attached coloured silk tassels that blew about in the wind in a most agreeable manner ... ' Clavijo goes on to tell of the innumerable other wonders of the palace: the solid gold tables and the golden flasks and cups, set with pearls and emeralds and

*In Chagatai Turkish the word for pig is variously *Tanguz*, *Tunguz* or *Donguz*.

turquoises and rubies; and of Tamerlane's rage when, owing to the idleness of a dragoman, Clavijo and his party arrived late for dinner; and the terrible punishment that was almost inflicted on the unfortunate dragoman. His nose, it seems, was to be pierced and he was to be led about the camp by a cord, 'a warning to all'. And finally the 'five sheep and two great jars of wine' which Tamerlane sent to his guests to make up for having missed dinner.

A week later, on Monday 22 September, the envoys were entertained by Tamerlane in an even more magnificent palace, 'much the finest of any that we had visited hitherto, and in the ornamentation of its buildings, in the gold and blue tile work far the most sumptuous'. This was known as *Bagh-i-Naw*, the New Garden, and here the wine flowed freely. 'It is the custom with the Tartars', writes Clavijo, 'to drink their wine before eating and they then drink so copiously and so often that they get very drunk. No feast, we were informed, was regarded as a real festival unless the guests drank themselves silly.' Again there was the usual vast quantity of roast horse-flesh and boiled mutton, and a robe of gold brocade for Clavijo and for each of his companions.

Next day yet another invitation arrived to yet another feast at yet another palace. 'Both the garden and the palace were very fine', writes Clavijo, 'and Timur seemed in excellent humour, drinking much wine and making his guests do the same. There was, further, an abundance of meat to eat, both of horse-flesh and mutton, as is ever their custom.' And, of course, the usual robes of cloth of gold and a throng of guests so great that the guards had to force a passage to let the Castilians pass, and the dust, that fine, light, powdery dust of Central Asia, 'was blown up so thick that our faces and clothing became all of one colour and covered by it'.

'The various orchards and palaces above mentioned belonging to His Highness,' writes Clavijo, 'stand close up to the city of Samarkand, while stretching beyond lies the great plain with open fields through which the river flows, being diverted into many watercourses.' It was in this plain that at the beginning of October Tamerlane ordered a gathering of the Great Horde, 'each tribe taking up its appointed place', with twenty thousand tents 'pitched in regular streets all round the Royal Camp', and as many more spread over the surrounding plain, and more tribes coming in every day from the outlying districts, and butchers and cooks and bakers and even bath attendants to minister to their needs. Meanwhile, Tamerlane, concerned, as ever, for the well-being of his Spanish guests, had sent them 'ten sheep and a horse, to supply the banquet with meat, also a full charge of wine, and we dined very sumptuously.'

When the Great Horde had assembled, Tamerlane 'gave orders for a grand feast', or rather a series of grand feasts, which seem to have continued right through October, one of their purposes being to celebrate a number of royal weddings, notably the nuptials of six of his grandsons, including Ulug Beg and Ibrahim Sultan, the sons of his son Shakh Rukh. Clavijo describes at length the various tents and pavilions of the Royal Camp that were now erected by the banks of the Zeravshan, including one that was entirely lined with ermine. On reaching the royal camp, he himself was 'left for a season to rest in the shade under a spacious awning ... made of white linen overset and let in with coloured embroidery ... and fashioned long and high in order to be open to the sun and catch the breeze'. Near this awning was the great square pavilion, a hundred yards wide and a hundred yards long, in which Tamerlane himself sat when giving audience. The ceiling of the pavilion was circular, forming a dome, and was supported by twelve great tent-poles painted in blue and gold, from which hung silk curtains, looped back so as to form arch-ways, the whole structure being supported by five hundred red ropes, and the inner walls lined with magnificently embroidered crimson tapestry and silk of many colours worked with gold thread. At the four corners of the ceiling, 'its mark of greatest beauty', were wrought four eagles sitting with folded wings, while the outer walls of the pavilion were made of silk woven in bands of white and black and yellow. At each corner was set a tall pole topped by a globe of burnished copper bearing a crescent, and in the centre four more supported 'a kind of silken turret with simulated battlements', so that 'from a distance this great tent would seem to be a castle, it is so immensely broad and high'. It was, says Clavijo, 'a wonder to behold and magnificent beyond description'.

The pavilion, he goes on to tell us, stood within the *Sararpardeh* or Royal Enclosure, a high wall of patterned silk, 'as it might be the wall of a town or castle', with an arched gateway in it. Nearby were other great enclosures, containing more tents and pavilions, all made from different coloured silks and tapestries. From high up, in the cupola of one of these swooped a great silver-gilt eagle with wings extended, while a fathom and a half below, as though in flight from the eagle, were three falcons, also in silver gilt, with their wings spread and their heads turned back to look at him. 'They are set here', writes Clavijo, 'as though some special purpose were intended'. Two of the enclosures, 'each of its own colour and design' with many more tents within them, were allotted to Tamerlane's two principal wives, his chief wife, the Great Khanum, and his second wife, the Kuchik Khanum or Little Lady. His remaining six wives (for he had eight at this time, twice the number strictly allowed by Moslem law) were accommodated elsewhere in other parts of the camp.

And now the celebrations began. At midday on Monday 6 October Tamerlane entered the Royal Enclosure and proceeded to his Great Pavilion, 'whither he sent and had us brought ... and we dined on mutton and horse-flesh, with the usual abundance'. From now onwards for the rest of the month there seems to have been a banquet every day, except once, when 'a great wind arose, blowing fiercely'. On Thursday 9 October Clavijo was invited to a splendid feast given by Khanzadeh, Timur's favourite daughter-in-law, the widow of his son Jahangir, 'a Princess now some forty years of age, fair of complexion and fat'. This seems to have been a most cheerful occasion. Even before dinner was served 'many of the men sitting before the Princess were beginning to show signs of being in their cups and a number were dead drunk'. On the appearance of the boiled mutton and roast horse-flesh, 'all began to eat with much talking and joking, one snatching a piece of meat from another and all the guests were very merry'. 'The amount of mutton and horse-meat they did eat that day', says Clavijo, 'was enormous and they drank wine and were exceedingly merry ... And all the ladies', he tells us, 'likewise partook of the wine', drinking turn about with the men, who presented their wine to them in gold cups, 'laughing merrily' at the amount the gentlemen drank, for 'at none of their feasts do they consider hilarity is attained unless many guests are properly in drink'.

Considering that they were by religion total abstainers, wine seems to have played an important part in the daily life of Tamerlane and his court. Sometimes, 'the sooner to enjoy drunkenness', spirits were served as well as wine, and Clavijo has left us a convivial picture of another occasion when 'the drinking was such that all when they left the feast were besotted drunk, His Majesty finally remaining all alone in his tent in a state of much cheerfulness and contentment'.

For storing all the wine, a special field was kept near the Royal Enclosure, the great sixty-gallon jars being placed at intervals all round the field. Should anyone come near the jars, they were at once shot at or struck down by guards armed with bows and arrows and maces. 'We noticed', says Clavijo, 'that many had thus been wounded for their inadvertence and some had been thrown out for dead and were lying at the gates of the enclosure.'

At one of Tamerlane's feasts all eight of his wives were present. The Great Khanum was the first to make her appearance. She wore an outer robe of red silk embroidered with gold. Her long train was carried by fifteen ladies-in-waiting who walked behind her. Her face was painted dead white, like a mask. Before it she wore a fine white veil, and on her head a scarlet helmet-shaped head-dress, ornamented with gigantic pearls and rubies and turquoises and other precious stones and supporting an immense plume of white feathers. 'As she came forward', writes Clavijo, 'this mighty headgear waved back and forth and the Princess was wearing all her hair loose, hanging down over her shoulders, dead black in colour, the hue they most esteem.' Around the Princess walked numerous ladies-in-waiting, supporting her head-dress. To Clavijo she seemed to have round about her as many as three hundred attendants. Over her head a servant carried a white silk parasol, domed like the top of a tent and supported by a pole the size of a lance, holding it with immense care so as to keep the sun off her face. In front of her and her ladies marched a great number of eunuchs. On entering the Pavilion where Tamerlane was already seated, the Great Khanum seated herself beside, but slightly behind him, while three ladies steadied her head-dress. Once the First Lady was seated, the Second Lady made her appearance, coming from her own enclosure. She, too, wore robes of red and a similar head-dress with many jewels, and many ladies in attendance, and took her seat slightly behind the first. Next, in their proper order, came the Third, Fourth, Fifth, Sixth, Seventh, and Eighth Wives. The Eighth Timur had only married a month or two before and to her, Clavijo learned, he had given the name of *Jawhar Aga*, or Queen of Hearts.

Besides eating and drinking, Tamerlane devised numerous entertainments for the benefit of his guests: wrestlers, acrobats, performing elephants and horses, which 'ended with the elephants running about, pursuing the people assembled in the crowds around and about'. After which the elephants all charged abreast and the earth shook at their onrush.

On another occasion Tamerlane gave orders for all the merchants and traders of Samarkand, jewellers, cooks, butchers, bakers, tailors and shoe-makers to come out to the meadows where the Great Horde was encamped and there offer their goods for sale and each give a display of his particular trade or craft. And in among all the traders' booths and display tents he had a great gallows set up, explaining that, while wishing to give pleasure to the common people, he also wanted to issue a warning and make an example of those who had offended him. The first to be hanged was the Mayor of Samarkand, who, Tamerlane said, had betrayed his trust and oppressed the people. Then a friend and associate of the Mayor's, and, after torture, one of his own courtiers who had interceded on behalf of the Mayor, offering Tamerlane a vast sum (which he had at once accepted) if he would only spare him. And, finally, in spite of all his promises and protestations, a great lord of the court who had been put in charge of Tamerlane's stud and could not now account for all the three thousand horses entrusted to his care. 'It is', observes Clavijo, 'the custom among these Tartars, if the culprit be a person of rank, to put him to death by hanging, but if he be a man of the people, they behead, for they hold decapitation to be a dreadful deed and a matter of much dishonour.'

Once Clavijo and his companions were invited to dine by the Great Khanum, and afterwards taken to see her treasures. Among these were the great double doors of her tent, plated with silver gilt ornamented with blue enamel with insets in gold. On one door Saint Peter was represented and on the other Saint Paul, each saint with a book in his hands and both made of silver. Both, it seemed, came from a Christian church at Brusa and had been taken from Sultan Bayazid after his defeat at Ankara two years before. Clavijo was also shown an ornamental cabinet made of solid gold encrusted with jewels and filled with gold plates and cups and goblets; and a low gold table, with a great emerald set in the top; and a tree, as tall as a man, also made of gold, with vast numbers of rubies and emeralds and turquoises, and great round pearls as fruit, and numerous little birds made from gold enamel, some seeming ready to fly, and some just alighted, and some pecking at the rubies and emeralds.

Finally, on Thursday 30 October Timur returned to the city of Samarkand, and there took up his residence near a mosque which he was having built as a mausoleum for his favourite grandson and successor designate, Muhammad Sultan, who had died of wounds received in the great battle against Bayazid. The original building had not been to Timur's liking, and, after visiting the site in a litter, for he could no longer ride a horse, he had ordered it to be demolished and rebuilt within ten days. This the builders, in fear for their lives, had somehow accomplished by the appointed date, and when Clavijo went to see it, the lofty structure with its fine blue and gold tiles was already complete. Its fluted turquoise dome rose from an octagonal base. On either side of the entrance stood twin minarets. The walls within were lined with alabaster and green marble. It was (and still is) one of the most beautiful buildings in the world, and Tamerlane, who was to be buried in it himself, was presumably at last satisfied with it. At the ensuing celebration the quantity of roast meat consumed was, Clavijo tells us, 'immense'; the envoys received more cloth-of-gold robes and Tamerlane assured them that he now regarded the King of Spain with as much affection as his own son.

No sooner had the mosque in honour of his grandson been completed, than Tamerlane embarked on a fresh project: the building of a great new bazaar to accommodate and display all the rich merchandise coming into the city 'from Cathay, India, Tartary and many quarters beside'. His orders were 'that a street should be built to pass straight through Samarkand, with shops on either side of it in which every kind of merchandise should be sold, going right through from one side of the City to the other side ... This task he entrusted to two great nobles at the same time letting them know that they would pay with their heads for any delay. These nobles therefore began at speed, causing all houses to be torn down along the line indicated by His Majesty. No heed was paid to complaints from the owners of property. No sooner had all the houses been thrown down than the master builders came and laid out the broad new street, erecting shops on the one side and opposite, placing before each a high stone bench that was topped with white slabs. Each shop had two chambers, front and back, and the street way was arched over with a domed roof in which were windows to let the light through. As soon as these shops were made ready forthwith they were occupied by merchants selling goods of all sorts: and at intervals down the street were erected water fountains. The cost of all this work', we learn, 'was charged to the town council and workmen did not lack, as many coming forward as were wanted by the overseers. The masons who worked through the day at night all went home, their places being taken by as many as had gone, who worked throughout the night hours. Some would be pulling down the houses while others laid out the roadway, others again building anew, and the tumult was such day and night that it seemed all the devils of hell were at work here. Thus in the course of twenty days the whole new street was carried through: a wonder indeed to behold; but those whose houses had been thus demolished had good cause to complain.'

Clavijo tells us that the vast mosque which Tamerlane had built in memory of one of his mothers-in-law seemed to him and to his companions the noblest in all Samarkand. But Tamerlane was dissatisfied with the entrance gate, which he said was too low and must at once be pulled down and rebuilt, and, being in poor health, had himself carried every morning to the building site in his litter to supervise the work and urge on the workmen, throwing down cooked meat and coins to the men working on the foundations to encourage them, 'as though one should cast bones to dogs in a pit'.

But by now the old man's health was failing fast, and when at the beginning of November the envoys requested an audience in order to take leave of him, they were repeatedly put off by agitated courtiers and finally told in so many words that Tamerlane was dying, and that, for their own sakes, they had better be off before the announcement of his death threw his empire into turmoil. This advice they in the end reluctantly accepted, leaving Samarkand on 21 November without another audience and without the letters they had been promised for King Henry.

In fact, Tamerlane recovered sufficiently to spend December assembling his armies for the next campaign he had planned, namely an invasion of China undertaken for the purpose of punishing the 'Pig-Emperor' for his insolence in sending an ambassador to demand tribute of him. In January 1405 he set out to march across Central Asia, and in early February crossed the frozen Jaxartes. But at Otrar his sickness returned to him, and on the seventeenth day of that month he died at the age of sixty-nine.

The news of Tamerlane's death overtook Clavijo and his companions some weeks later at Tabriz, and their departure from Persia was delayed for several more months by the civil war which now broke out. In the end, however, after numerous adventures, they managed to reach Trebizond, and here safely boarded a Genoese ship bound for Pera with a cargo of hazel-nuts. Seville they were finally to reach in the spring of 1406, nearly three years after they had set out.

Another account of Tamerlane's death comes from Johann Schiltberger, a fifteen-year-old German squire from Bavaria, who had first been taken prisoner by the Turks with his knight at Nikopolis and, having subsequently fallen into Tamerlane's hands after the latter's victory over Bayazid at Ankara, remained in his service and that of his successors for a considerable number of years. Schiltberger attributes Tamerlane's death partly to irritation at the insolence of the Emperor of China, but partly also to jealousy and disappointment at the conduct of his youngest wife, presumably the 'Queen of Hearts', mentioned by Clavijo. 'When Tamerlin came home', says Schiltberger, 'his eldest wife told him that his youngest wife had cared for one of his vassals and had broken her vow. He could not believe it. She came to him and said: "Come to her and order her to open her trunk: you will find a ring with a precious stone, and a letter which he has sent her." Tamerlin sent to tell her that he would pass the night with her, and when he came into her room, he told her to open her trunk. This was done, and he found the ring and the letter. He sat down near her, and asked when the ring and the letter had come to her? She fell at his feet, and begged he would not be angry, because one of his vassals had sent them to her without any right. After this he went out of the room, and ordered that she should be immediately beheaded. This was done. He then sent five thousand horsemen after this same vassal, that they might bring him as a prisoner; but he was warned by the commander who was sent after him, and the vassal took with him five hundred men, his wife and children, and fled to the country of Massandaran. There Tamerlin could not get at him. It fretted him so much that he had killed his wife and that the vassal had escaped, that he died, and was buried in the country with great magnificence. Be it also known', Schiltberger continues, 'that after he was buried, the priests that belonged to the temple heard him howl every night during a whole year. His friends gave large alms, that he should cease his howlings. But this was of no use. They asked advice of their priests, and went to his son and begged that he would set free the prisoners taken by his father in other countries, and especially those that were in his capital, who were all craftsmen he had brought to his capital, where they had to work. He let them go, and so soon as they were free Tamerlin did not howl any more.'

'All that is written above', adds Schiltberger with conviction, 'happened during the six years that I was with Tamerlin and I also was present.'

6 *The Roles Reversed*

After the brief period of internecine strife described by Clavijo, Tamerlane was succeeded by his younger son, Shakh Rukh, a devout Moslem and a man of peace, whose long reign of more than forty years made possible the consolidation of Timur's empire and its conversion into an orthodox Moslem Khanate with its centre in Khorasan. Mawarannahr, meanwhile, was governed as a part of this empire by Shakh Rukh's son Ulug Beg, a man of wide learning and culture, whose studies in the field of astronomy were centuries ahead of his time and who endowed Samarkand and Bokhara with some of their finest buildings. On Shakh Rukh's death in 1447, Ulug Beg succeeded briefly to his father's throne, but was murdered two years later by his own son, Abd al-Latif, who at the same time further secured his position by murdering his brother Abd al-Aziz. Shortly afterwards Abd al-Latif was himself murdered by his cousin Abdullah, who was then overthrown by another cousin, Abu Said, one of the ablest members of his family. Abu Said managed to survive until 1469, when he was killed by yet another cousin in revenge for the execution of the latter's mother, Shakh Rukh's favourite wife.

Over the next two or three hundred years this pattern was constantly to recur, and Central Asia became the scene of a prolonged struggle for power. In the lands between the Oxus and the Jaxartes power had passed to the Uzbeks under their leader Mohammed Shaibani, a descendant of Jenghiz Khan's grandson, Shaiban. Mohammed Shaibani was a considerable military leader, who by the year 1500 had taken Bokhara and Samarkand and made himself master of all Mawarannahr. Ten years later he was dead, killed in battle at Merv, and his skull, set in gold, had been made into a drinking cup for the Shah of Iran. But by one means or another the Shaibanid dynasty he founded was to hold sway in Mawarannahr for the next hundred years, making it the national home of the Uzbeks, as is recognized by its present name of Uzbekistan.

The attempts of the Shaibanids to extend their dominions at the expense of their neighbours southwards beyond the Amu Darya, the Elburz, or the Paropamisus were, however, unsuccessful. As a result, the Uzbeks became isolated from the rest of the Islamic world, their isolation being intensified by the fact that they belonged to the Sunni sect, while their Persian neighbours were Shiahs. But, though cut off from current Moslem philosophical and theological trends, they continued to build in Samarkand and Bokhara handsomely decorated mosques and medressehs (religious colleges) in a style not unworthy of their predecessors. Racially, meanwhile, the Uzbeks, like the other nomads of Mongol origin, were becoming increasingly assimilated to the native Turkish and Iranian stock of the oases.

Already the opening of the oceanic trade-routes had lessened the importance of the transcontinental caravan trade which for so long had been Central Asia's principal source of prosperity and had made it a meeting-place for traders and travellers from Europe, the Middle East and China. Now, Vasco da Gama's circumnavigation of Africa and the opening up of the sea-route between Europe and the Far East led to its further decline. And this, too, increased Mawarannahr's isolation from the rest of the world.

Only a very few travellers from the West managed to reach Central Asia at this time. One was the British merchant-adventurer, Anthony Jenkinson, who set out for Bokhara from Moscow in April 1558 with a cargo of English cloth and other merchandise, and with letters of recommendation from Ivan the Terrible whose active interest in Tartary was already beginning to manifest itself in a number of ways. Jenkinson's account of his expedition gives a good idea of the hazards and hardships which the journey now involved. From Moscow he and two other Englishmen, Richard and Robert Johnson, travelled by river to Astrakhan, where, having reached the limit of the Tsar's dominions, they bought a ship to carry them across the Caspian Sea. But half-way across, their ship was boarded by thirty 'gentlemen, banished from their countrey, and out of living', who 'came to see if there were any Russes or other Christians in our barke', and, in the event, the travellers were only saved from slavery or worse by the benevolence and ready wit of a 'holy Tartar', who swore black and blue that they were all good Moslems. The inhabitants of the eastern shore of the Caspian they found on arrival to be 'very badde and brutish people, for they ceased not dayly to molest us either by fighting, stealing or begging, raysing the prise of horse and camels, and victuals double, and forced us to buy the water that wee did drinke'.

But their troubles in fact had scarcely begun. Five days' journey farther on they encountered 'certain Tartars on horseback', who 'stayed our caravan in the name of their prince, and opened our wares, and took such things as they thought best for their said prince without money'. There followed '20 days in the wilderness from the sea side without seeing towne or habitation, carying provision of victuals with us for the same time, and were driven by necessitie to eate one of my camels and a horse, and during the said 20 dayes we found no water, but such as we drewe out of olde deepe wells, being very brackish and salt, and yet sometimes passed two or three dayes without the same'. After this there was another encounter with brigands. 'They willed us', writes Jenkinson, 'to yeeld ourselves, but wee defied them, wherewith they shotte at us all at once, and wee at them very hotly and so continued our fight from morning untill two hourse within night, divers men, horses and camels being wounded and slaine on both partes: and had it not been for 4 hand gunnes which I and my company had and used, we had been overcome and destroyed'.

At last, on 23 December 1558, Jenkinson reached the 'great Citie' of Bokhara with its 'high walls of earth, with divers gates into the same' and its 'many houses, temples and monuments of stone sumptuously builded and gilt'. The King, to whom, as the Tsar's Ambassador, he formally presented his letters, 'interteined us', he writes, 'most gently, and caused us to eat in his presence, and divers times he sent for me and devised with me familiarly in his secret chamber, as well of the power of the Emperour, and the great Turke, as also of our countreis, lawes, and religion'. 'But', adds the merchant-adventurer, 'after all this great intertainment he shewed himselfe a very Tartar: for he went to the warres owing me money, and sawe mee not paid before his departure.'

Jenkinson's return journey to Moscow was no less adventurous. After narrowly escaping 'the danger of 400 rovers, which lay in waite for us back againe', he found, on reaching the Caspian, that his barque now had 'neither anker, cable, cocke nor saile'. Having 'made us a sail of cloth of cotton wooll and rigged our barke as well as we could', he and his companions finally set sail, and after passing 'in this voyage various fortunes, arrived at last 'in safetie at Astracan'. 'Note', writes Jenkinson, 'that during the time of our navigation, wee sette uppe the redde crosse of S. George' in our flagges ... which I suppose was never seene in the Caspian sea before.'* On his return to Moscow, one year, five months and nine days

---

*It was to reappear there briefly more than 350 years later, at the end of the First World War when a few British gunboats operated out of Baku.

E

after he had set out, Jenkinson dined in state at the Kremlin with Ivan the Terrible, who 'sent him meate by a Duke' and questioned him graciously about the countries he had visited, while he, for his part, gave the Emperor 'a white cowe's taile of Cathay and a drumme of Tartaria, which he well accepted'.

Under the Janids, who succeeded the Shaibanids in 1599 and from Bokhara governed most of Mawarannahr for nearly two hundred years, this country's isolation was further intensified. Nor was there any change under the Mangits, who succeeded the Janids at the end of the eighteenth century. In the neighbouring Khanates of Khiva, as Khorezm was now called, and Kokand, other independent monarchs held sway, bickering spasmodically with their neighbours and, like them, cut off from all contact with the outside world. To make things worse, tribes of fierce Turkmen nomads now ranged freely over the deserts east of the Caspian, attacking such lines of communication as there were, raiding caravans, selling their prisoners as slaves, and admitting allegiance to no one.

Meanwhile, far away to the north and west beyond the deserts, what remained of the Golden Horde had long since begun to disintegrate. Already in the middle of the fifteenth century it had broken up into a number of independent Tartar Khanates, at Kazan, at Astrakhan on the Volga, in the Crimea, to the north of the Caspian and in the Irtysh–Tobol basin of Siberia, all perpetually at odds one with another and all increasingly threatened by their neighbours the Russians.

In the great days of the Golden Horde, the subject Russian princes had, as we have seen, readily paid tribute to their Mongol overlords and had been allowed in return to retain their national identity. A century later, in 1332, Uzbek, who ruled over the Golden Horde from 1313 to 1340 and according to some authorities gave his name to the Uzbek race, had granted the title of Grand Duke to Ivan I of Muscovy, on condition that he kept his turbulent neighbours in order. Ivan and his successors made good use of the authority given them by the Khan's mandate to consolidate their own position at the expense of their neighbours. For Muscovy it was the first step towards ultimate supremacy. With the disruption of the Golden Horde and its fragmentation into mutually hostile Khanates, it became increasingly easy during the second half of the fifteenth and first half of the sixteenth centuries for the Muscovites, whose power was now growing apace, to play off their former overlords against each other and assert their own predominance. In 1552 Ivan the Terrible captured Kazan, and two years later stormed Astrakhan, subsequent Tartar uprisings and rebellions being put down with the utmost ferocity. In 1583, on the Tsar's orders (for the rulers of Russia had now assumed this title), an army under the Cossack leader Yermak was sent by the Stroganov family of merchant princes* to capture the town of Sibir and overthrow the Tartar Khan of Western Siberia, and not many years later the first Russian pioneers, pushing on across Siberia, finally reached the shores of the Pacific. Henceforward the Tartar Khans, in so far as they existed at all, became Russian puppets. The roles were now reversed. It was left to Catherine the Great, two hundred years later, in 1783, to occupy and annex the last remaining Tartar Khanate of the Crimea, which had only survived until then as a Turkish protectorate.

Having pushed down the Volga and conquered Siberia, the Russians were now starting ('smoothly, glidingly', wrote Gogol) to turn their attention southwards to Central Asia. And here again the resistance they encountered, though sometimes fierce, was in the main not very formidable. By the beginning of the eighteenth century the Tsars had established a loose suzerainty over the various nomad Khans who ruled over the Kazak and Kirghiz tribes of Southern Siberia, Semirechiye and the Syr Darya region. During the first half of the nineteenth century they followed this up by annexation and, in suitable areas, colonization by Russian settlers, any resistance being ruthlessly repressed. By 1854, reaching down southwards from Semipalatinsk, they had established themselves at Vierny (now Alma Ata) at the foot of the Tien Shan, on the borders of Chinese Turkestan.

Further west, the Russians were poised for the conquest of Turkestan. Already under Peter the Great two or three expeditions had set out across the Transcaspian steppes to invade Turkestan, but had met with disaster and been forced to turn back before reaching their objective. More recently in 1840 General Perovski had led a strong expedition against Khiva from Orenburg, but this too had been a failure.

The next Russian campaign was better prepared. Turkestan was at this time divided between three weak independent states, constantly bickering among themselves: Khiva (the ancient Khorezm), Bokhara, and Kokand. In 1855 the Russians seized from the Khan of Kokand the fort of Ak Mechet, later Perovsk, on the Syr Darya and dug themselves in along the

*The originators of that famous Russian dish *bœuf Stroganov*.

river. Meanwhile the capture of Vierny the year before had, as we have already seen, given them another base further east. For the time being Russian military operations in Central Asia were held up by the Crimean War and by the long-drawn-out campaign the Russians were fighting in the Caucasus. But in the spring of 1864 operations were resumed in Central Asia, and in May of that year a force of some 2,600 men commanded by Colonel Cherniayev set out from Vierny, while another column of 1,600 men under Colonel Veryovkin started from Perovsk. In June Cherniayev's force seized Aulie Ata, while Veryovkin took the town of Yasi (or Turkestan). The two columns then joined forces under Cherniayev, and in September stormed the citadel of Chimkent, routing the native garrison of 10,000 men for the loss of only two Russians.

To the great powers, the Russians had, in November 1863, addressed a circular signed by their Foreign Minister, Prince Gorchakov. In this they had explained, not very convincingly, that they were only securing their frontiers. But now Cherniayev, though officially under orders to advance no further, took it upon himself to attack and capture the Kokandi city of Tashkent. In order to reassure the British, who, alarmed at the threat to India, were by now showing signs of serious concern at the Russian advance, Cherniayev was recalled (and at once promoted), but his successor General Romanovski started where he had left off, first invading Bokharan territory in the spring of 1866 and then decisively defeating the Khan of Kokand, who now sued for peace and agreed to acknowledge himself a Russian vassal. Finally on 11 July 1867 an Imperial Decree established the Governorate-General of Turkestan, with Tashkent as its capital and embracing all the territories occupied since 1847. Of this General K. P. von Kaufmann, a man of outstanding ability, was appointed to be the first Governor-General, with wide military and political powers.

General Kaufmann lost no time in making his presence felt in Central Asia. In the spring of 1868, on a suitable pretext, he invaded the territory of the Emir of Bokhara. On 2 May he took Samarkand and, pushing southwards into the foothills, occupied Urgut and Katta Kurgan. On 2 June he encountered and routed the main Bokharan force on the heights of Zerabulak not far from Katta Kurgan. By a peace treaty signed a fortnight later, the Emir of Bokhara ceded Samarkand and the surrounding areas to the Russians and agreed that what was left of his country should become a Russian protectorate.

After an incursion in 1871 into Chinese Turkestan (from which they eventually withdrew), the Russians next turned their attention to the Khanate of Khiva. Previous Russian expeditions had been defeated by the waterless deserts surrounding the oasis. This time Kaufmann left nothing to chance. The expedition was mounted with the utmost care. The Russian force numbered 13,000, with sixty-two guns, and was divided into four columns. The main column, under Kaufmann himself, was to start from Tashkent; another from Orenburg; and two more from the East Caspian ports of Krasnovodsk and Fort Alexandrovski. The British Government were officially informed that only punitive action was intended in retaliation for Khivan border raids. And in May 1873 the expedition set out.

The column from Krasnovodsk suffered so much from heat and lack of water that it was obliged to turn back. But by the end of May the other three columns had reached their objectives, and on 10 June the walled city of Khiva fell almost without a fight. A couple of months later, on 12 August, while several thousand miles away the more sporting members of Mr Gladstone's government were setting out for the moors, secure in the belief that they had nothing to worry about in Central Asia, General Kaufmann and the Khan of Khiva sat down together to sign a treaty by which the latter ceded a large part of his territory to the Russians and placed the remainder under Russian protection.

An eye-witness, the American journalist, J. A. MacGahan, has described the Khan's first interview with Kaufmann in the garden of his own palace. Dismounting while still some distance away, Mohammed Rahim Khan advanced on foot, tall sheepskin hat in hand, bowing low to Kaufmann as he approached. A big man, of about thirty, well over six feet tall and heavily built, with a rather crooked aquiline nose, a heavy sensual mouth and a thin black beard and moustache, he had a frightened look and, as he knelt on the ground before Kaufmann, a fair, slightly built figure on a camp stool, he could scarcely look the Russian in the face.

'Well, Khan,' said Kaufmann with a gentle smile, which did not altogether disguise his satisfaction, 'you see, I have come to see you at last, as I wrote you I would, three years ago.'

'Yes, Allah has willed it.'

'No, Khan, there you are mistaken. Allah had very little to do with it. You have brought it upon yourself. If you had listened to my counsel three years ago, and acceded to my just demands, you would not have seen me here. In other words, if you had done as I advised you, Allah would not have willed it.'

'The pleasure of seeing the *Yarim-Padshah* is so great, that I could wish nothing changed.'

'The pleasure, I assure you, Khan, is mutual. But now let us proceed to business.'

Further east, in Kokand, the reigning Khan had in practice been a Russian vassal since 1865. In 1875, however, a rebellion broke out in his territories and a rebel force, numbering about 40,000 men, chased him out and attacked the Russian garrison. Apprised of the situation, General Kaufmann again acted with speed and resolution. Marching on Kokand, he routed the rebels, put them to flight, massacred the fugitives, re-occupied the main towns, and on 19 February finally annexed Kokand to Russia, restoring to his new province its ancient name of Ferghana.

Between the frontiers of Russia on the one hand and those of Persia and Afghanistan on the other there now only remained the desolate region known today as Turkmenistan and in Tsarist days as Transcaspia. This was inhabited by the unruly Tekke-Turkomans, the most notorious marauders in Central Asia. Since 1869 the Russians had held the port of Krasnovodsk on the Caspian, which, for administrative purposes, was included in the Governorship-General of the Caucasus. From this base, in September 1879 a strong Russian force set out across the desert to attack the Turkoman stronghold of Geok Tepe. They were, however, driven off by the Turkomans with heavy losses. A second expedition was now mounted, under the command of the famous General Skobelyov, who, after distinguishing himself under Kaufmann in Central Asia, had won fresh glory fighting the Turks in the Balkans: *Akh Pasha*, they called him, the White General. To Skobelyov war was the highest expression of human energy. 'He rode to battle', writes a contemporary, 'clad in white, decked with orders, scented and curled, like a bridegroom to a wedding, his eyes gleaming with wild delight, his voice tremulous with joyous excitement.' *Guenz Kanli* was the name the Turkomans gave him—Bloody Eyes.

In January 1881, having assembled a force of over 7,000 men, Skobelyov launched his attack on Geok Tepe and took it by storm, slaughtering many thousands of Turkoman men, women and children in the process, and thousands more in the rout and pursuit that followed. 'All who had not succeeded in escaping were killed to a man by the Russian soldiers', wrote his Chief of Staff. For eleven miles the Russians, with horse, foot and cannon, hunted the panic-stricken throng of fugitives, killing another eight thousand men, women and children. 'They lay', wrote an eye-witness, 'in rows like freshly mown hay, as they had been swept down by the *mitrailleuses* and cannon.' In all no less than twenty thousand Turkomans were killed, for the loss of fewer than three hundred Russians. 'I hold it', wrote Skobelyov, 'as a principle that in Asia the duration of peace is in direct proportion to the slaughter you inflict upon the enemy. The harder you hit them, the longer they will stay quiet afterwards.' This time, certainly, his method worked, and on 6 May 1881 the whole of Transcaspia was annexed to Russia.

Three years later, in 1884, the Russians rounded off their Central Asian conquests by occupying the oases of Merv and Sarakhs, and the following year their patrols actually brushed with the Afghans at Kushk. In Great Britain the fall of Merv and the events that followed gave rise to an attack of what the Duke of Argyll wittily termed 'Mervousness', and for a time it looked as though serious trouble might ensue between the two countries, whose respective spheres of interest in Central Asia were now only divided by a few miles of rock and desert. In the end, however, a *modus vivendi* was arrived at, and within a few years the course of events elsewhere in the world had made allies of the erstwhile rivals.

Russia's conquest of Central Asia was now complete. Her territories marched with those of China to the east and Afghanistan and Persia to the south. At one point in the High Pamirs they were barely separated by a narrow strip of Afghan territory from the borders of British India. Of the independent khanates and emirates with which Central Asia had once abounded, only Bokhara and Khiva survived, both as Russian protectorates.

With the outbreak of the Bolshevik Revolution in 1917 and the ensuing civil war, Central Asia was again thrown into turmoil. Briefly, Bokhara and Khiva enjoyed a new period of independence until in the end both were once more absorbed by Soviet Russia. In some areas resistance to the Bolsheviks flared up briefly in the nineteen-twenties and was ruthlessly repressed. Finally, under the federal system subsequently evolved by Stalin, five Soviet Socialist Republics were eventually created in Central Asia—Kazakstan, Kirghisia, Uzbekistan, Tajikstan and Turkmenistan—each endowed with its own government and Communist Party, and possessing in theory the right to secede from the Union, but each in practice taking its orders on all major issues from Moscow.

7 *Kazaks and Kirghiz*

Of the present Central Asian Republics of the Union by far the largest is the vast Soviet Socialist Republic of Kazakstan, sprawling right across the north of Central Asia, from the frontiers of European Russia and the shores of the Caspian in the West to the borders of China in the East. Comprising much of what was once the territory of Batu's Golden Horde, it covers an area of a million square miles — more than the whole of Western Europe put together. Its population, on the other hand, amounts to only eight or nine million people, for much of its territory consists of desert — the fearsome waste of the Red Sands, or Kizil Kum, and of the Hungry Steppe.

My own first approach to Kazakstan and indeed to Central Asia was made more than thirty-five years ago. From Moscow I had travelled unobtrusively across Siberia as far as Novosibirsk and then turned suddenly southwards by the Turksib Railway. For a long way after leaving Novosibirsk, the landscape remained strictly Siberian: a flat plain covered with grey-green moss, enlivened by occasional clumps of silver birches. The change from Siberia to Central Asia came soon after entering Kazakstan, near Semipalatinsk. Now the railway track ran across a dreary expanse of desert, as flat, but far more desolate than the Siberian plain. At the halts along the line the peasants who rode in with food to sell to the passengers were no longer European Russians, but native Kazaks and Kirghiz with a strongly Asian cast of countenance: the women in strange, high, medieval-looking head-dresses; the men in long padded coats and skull-caps, or helmet-shaped cones of thick white felt with sharply upturned brims. Here and there you could see from the train the yurts, or circular skin tents, in which they lived.

Then, early one morning, as I looked out of the train window across the sandy waste, I saw something that filled me with excitement and delight. Far away to the south, dimly seen in the distance, towering high above the desert haze, rose a mighty range of mountains, their lower slopes veiled in cloud and vapours, their snow-clad peaks glittering in the sunlight, sus-

Into the Tien Shan

Alma Ata supermarket

◄ New Alma Ata

Old Alma Ata

◀ The kebab-seller

Alma Ata: Kazakstan

Making tea

In the Tien Shan

pended between earth and sky. These were the Tien Shan, the Mountains of Heaven. Beyond them lay China.

All day we trundled across the desert towards those distant peaks. Then, suddenly, in the early afternoon we found ourselves once again amid cultivation: apple orchards, the trees heavily laden with fruit; golden fields of Indian corn ripening in the sun; plantations of melons; rows of tall poplars growing by the side of canals and irrigation ditches. After the desert the foliage seemed lusciously, exuberantly green. We were nearing the city of Alma Ata.

Alma Ata is magnificently situated. Immediately behind it — an immensely dramatic backdrop — rise the snowy heights of the Tien Shan, part of the great mountain barrier which divides Russian Central Asia from Chinese Turkestan.

The city itself, the former Vierny, originally founded by the Russians in 1854 as a garrison town, is laid out in broad avenues of elms and poplars running at right angles to each other. When I first went there, before the last war, there were already a good many new buildings, and now there are even more: blocks of flats, department stores, an opera, a university, an imposing new government building, and more are going up all the time. But the green avenues of tall trees are still there, and the garrison church, where the soldiers of the Tsar once worshipped, and there are still enough of the old brightly painted wooden and stucco bungalows left, blue and white, pink and white, yellow and white, for the town not to have lost its pleasant bucolic character. In Kazak 'Alma Ata' means 'Father of Apples'. The name is well deserved, for the apples grown in the orchards which surround it are the finest both in size and flavour that I have tasted anywhere.

Under the Tsars what is now Kazakstan was a place of no great importance except as a military outpost. The Kazaks and Kirghiz who inhabited it were wandering nomad horsemen, who with their flocks and herds ranged over vast areas of country, pitching their circular skin tents where they could find pasture and possessing no fixed abode. By the turn of the century Vierny could still boast of no more than 20,000 or 30,000 inhabitants. Most of these were Russians. Its good climate and fruitfulness made it suitable for colonization by Europeans, and the Imperial Government encouraged peasants, retired soldiers and other European Russians to settle there, a policy that has been continued ever since. It was also a place to which political exiles were sent, notably Trotski, who, after his defeat by Stalin, spent a year or two there, before being finally expelled from the Soviet Union and ultimately tracked down and murdered in Mexico with an ice-axe.

Alma Ata's real significance dates back to the opening in 1931 of the Turksib Railway, which linked it up with the rest of the Soviet Union. By the time I reached it seven years later it was already a boom town. In those seven years its population had increased from 50,000 in 1931 to 230,000 in 1938. Today it is approaching a million. Of these the greater part are European Russians or Ukrainians, and only a minority native Kazaks. The latter vary considerably in type. Most of them have dark reddish-brown complexions and flat, round, moon-like faces with high Mongoloid cheek-bones and look rather like Eskimos, but some have oval faces with more aquiline features. Their language, like most of the native tongues of Soviet Central Asia, is akin to Turkish. Some of the peasants still wear their national dress, but in the towns European clothes, even among the native population, are becoming more usual. Though most of the Kazaks are now no longer nomads and have exchanged their tents for villages of mud huts, they are still born horsemen, naturally at home in the saddle.

Of recent years Kazakstan's economic importance has increased still further. It now produces more copper, lead and zinc than any other republic in the Union, and is third in production of coal and oil. It is also the biggest producer of sheep and cattle, and its grain production is in the neighbourhood of 16 million tons a year. This is partly the result of Khrushchev's Virgin Lands project, which, in a spectacular attempt to increase Soviet agricultural output, brought something like 100 million more acres under cultivation in Kazakstan and south-west Siberia.

Despite the restrained orientalism of some of its new buildings, Alma Ata remains a Russian town set down in the centre of Asia. But this seems to suit the Kazak portion of the population, who, forgetting their nomad past, parade up and down in their European suits looking pleased with themselves and with the amenities of their capital. In the middle of a neatly laid-out and well-kept public garden a magnificent equestrian statue has been erected to the memory of some Kazak national hero, who in 1916, just before the Bolshevik Revolution, led a revolt against the Russians and whose objectives, in theory at any rate, have now all been attained.

To suggest that the Kazaks have no say in running the affairs of their own Soviet Socialist Republic would be an exaggeration. On the contrary, the members of the Kazak Government and of the Alma Ata City Soviet, the Rector of the University of Kazakstan, the Chairman of the State Opera, the Director of the State Bank, the members of most of the principal commercial, industrial and agricultural enterprises in Kazakstan will, on inquiry, all be found to be native Kazaks. And, as far as local government is concerned, their views undoubtedly count for a good deal. There is even a Kazak Minister of Foreign Affairs, though what exactly his duties can be is less clear. But despite the decentralization which has undoubtedly taken place, Moscow is always on the end of the telephone. The ultimate decision, the ultimate authority, the ultimate power rests with Moscow. The Party line comes from Moscow, the troops are under the command of Moscow; and for Kazakstan, as for the other republics, the clause in its constitution enabling it to secede voluntarily from the Union remains as unreal as ever.

From Alma Ata the more enterprising traveller will somehow find his way at any rate into the foothills of the Tien Shan, known as the Ala Tau. I made the trip in an old-fashioned country bus and then on foot. At first, the countryside is outstandingly green and fertile, and the hamlets, for the most part inhabited by the descendants of the original Russian settlers, are set among orchards and well-cultivated fields. Then, as you climb, you come to pinewoods and Alpine pastures, and then, leaving the tree-line behind you, to the rocky snow-capped peaks of Kirghisia, the mountainous little Soviet Republic which forms a natural barrier between Soviet and Chinese Central Asia.

Soviet Kirghisia consists almost entirely of the massive mountain range rising to some 24,000 feet, which since 1860 has here formed the frontier between the Russian and Chinese Empires and still bears the Chinese name of Tien Shan. This merges further west into the even higher Pamirs of Soviet Tajikstan, which also borders briefly on China, though here the frontier has never been officially demarcated. Frunze, the capital of Kirghisia, called after a Russian hero of the Civil War, is an entirely modern Soviet city, complete with the usual opera house, university, and government buildings, which has sprung up in the foothills of the Tien Shan on the site of the Kirghiz village of Pishpek. Having arrived there not long ago at dawn and spent several hours inspecting it, I was quite ready to leave again by lunch-time. Though a pleasant enough place, with its solid modern buildings and leafy avenues, it had nothing whatever to distinguish it from any other new Soviet town.

Forty or fifty miles due south from Alma Ata in the mountains of Kirghisia is Issik Kol, an immense fresh-water lake, at least a hundred miles long and twenty or thirty miles wide. Tamerlane, it is said, had a favourite castle on its shores, and, according to legend, a whole city lies buried beneath its waters. Some say that here, in place of the lake, there was once a fruitful valley with towns full of happy and prosperous inhabitants: but the people were bewitched by an evil sorceress and lost all sense of shame, and the valley became a place of ill repute, which so enraged the gods that in due course they sent a great flood to destroy the valley and the towns and their inhabitants.

Others say that the town which was once there had only one fountain or spring, the key to which was kept by a holy man. One day, a young girl borrowed the key to the spring to draw water. But when she had opened it and the water had started to flow, a young man came along and took her away and made love to her, and in her rapture she forgot the key and the holy man and the flood she had let loose. And the water flowed and flowed and the valley was overwhelmed, and the town disappeared beneath the floods.

Issik Kol was already a lake in the days of the Buddhist monk Hsuang-tsang, who passed this way in the seventh century of our era. 'Dragons', he wrote, 'dwell in the waters of the lake.' Of dragons there are today no signs, though a local man I happened to meet there years ago told me that there were flamingoes in the neighbourhood. What is certain is that Issik Kol contains unmistakable evidence of an earlier, now submerged civilization. As recently as 1958 a Soviet archaeological expedition made interesting finds in its waters, including human remains, pottery and various other artifacts, and it is now generally agreed that the lake must have come into being suddenly and as the result of some tremendous natural upheaval. There is also evidence that a good many years ago this part of Central Asia sustained a large population of dinosaurs—which could have given rise to the tales of dragons.

Like their neighbours and cousins, the Kazaks, the Kirghiz were traditionally nomads and horsemen, living in round felt tents called yurts and migrating with their flocks and herds from winter to summer pastures and back again. Dark-skinned and black-haired, with slanting eyes and high cheek-bones, the Kirghiz, like the Kazaks, speak a language akin to Turkish, and the old men, whom you see in the villages and by the wayside and who ride into the towns to sell their produce in the markets, still wear national dress.

But in the towns Russian-style clothes are fast becoming the rule, and for most Kirghiz and Kazaks the nomad life is already a thing of the past. This transformation started in the 'twenties and 'thirties when collectivization and industrialization were the order of the day. At first these innovations were far from popular, and led at the time to tension and to a sharp fall in the livestock population of both Kirghisia and Kazakstan. Today only a few herdsmen and their families lead a half-nomad existence, up in the high mountains or out on the steppes, but still within the framework of state or collective farms, while the rest follow more settled agricultural or industrial pursuits in the villages and round the towns.

Another important change that has taken place has been in the balance of population, following intensive Russian colonization over the past hundred years or more. Under the Tsars, hundreds of thousands of Russians were settled in these frontier regions, and the process has continued since the Revolution. Today, in Kazakstan as a whole, Russians and Ukrainians account for more than half the population, greatly outnumbering the native Kazaks, who now amount to only a third of the total. And the same is true in Kirghisia.

This, in a sense, is the latest phase in a long-drawn-out process which began with the Mongol invasions of the Middle Ages, when the whole area was abruptly brought under the savage rule of Jenghiz Khan and his conquering hordes. It was then that the Kirghiz moved from the steppes of Siberia into the mountains of what is now Kirghisia, swept along before the onrush of the great invasions, while the Kazaks, for their part, stayed mainly in the plain. A hundred and fifty years later came Tamerlane, and after his death, as we have seen, the disintegration of his Central Asian empire into a collection of independent or semi-independent Moslem states, peopled by tribes of Turkic or Tartar race.

For centuries several thousands of miles still separated the dominions of the Grand Dukes and Tsars of Muscovy from those of the Emperors of China, and it was not until the middle of the nineteenth century that the rapid advance of Russia across Siberia and down into Central Asia brought the Tsar's victorious troops into sudden contact with the outposts of an already weakened Chinese Empire. It was then, by treaties signed in 1860 and 1881, that the frontiers of the two Empires were finally fixed — frontiers which, needless to say, were not unfavourable to Russia. On neither side of the new frontier was the native population either Russian or Chinese by race, but consisted for the most part of descendants of the original

Turko-Tartar inhabitants, and of the Mongol hordes who swept through and settled in Central Asia in the great racial upheavals of the Middle Ages. To these, on the Soviet side of the frontier, has been added a strong leavening of European Russians, while in Sinkiang reliable Chinese colonists are now beginning to account for a relatively high proportion of the total population.

Today the tension existing between China and the Soviet Union lends new interest to the whole area, and one is bound to ask oneself to what extent the native population in these frontier regions, some still claimed as part of China by the Chinese, who first occupied them in the eighth century A.D., might prove a liability to the Russians in the event of serious trouble between the two countries or of an attempt by China to mobilize the peoples of Asia against the Russian interlopers. To my mind hardly at all. It is true that the forced disruption of their tribal and nomad way of life after the Revolution and the collectivization of their livestock caused trouble at the time, but over the years they have been thoroughly Sovietized and brought into line. Besides, the nomad way of life is not without drawbacks and the economic development of the whole area has by now inevitably led to an enormous improvement in the general standard of living. As you stroll among the holiday crowds in the Park of Rest and Culture or watch a couple of Kazaks in a department store in Alma Ata hesitating between a choice of smartly cut business suits or a whole range of glossy furniture for their shiny new apartments, you feel that they probably don't miss their ancestral yurts all that much and are not too worried at not spending as many hours in the saddle and not owning as many sheep and goats as did their grandfathers. And their women even less. Nor can the tens of thousands of Kirghiz and Kazak refugees who fled across the frontier from Chinese Turkestan in the 'sixties in order to escape from the rigours of Chinese rule have been without their effect on local opinion and morale.

8 *Samarkand*

Neither Kazaks nor Kirghiz were ever very devout or very orthodox Mohammedans, having, like most Central Asian nomads, a tendency to lapse into a primitive Shamanist spirit- or devil-worship. Nor, as nomads, did they ever attain a very high level of civilization, and this has made their assimilation a relatively easy process. On the other hand, their neighbours the Uzbeks have a strong religious and cultural tradition, which goes back for centuries and has been much harder to break down. Bokhara, formerly the capital of the independent kingdom of that name, was, with Mecca and Medina, one of the holiest cities of the Moslem world. Elsewhere in the world, it was said, light came down from heaven; but from Bokhara it went up. For centuries both Bokhara and the neighbouring city of Samarkand were famous for their religious fanaticism, and less than a hundred years ago any Christian who found his way there stood a good chance of being tortured and killed. Few towns in the world were, as we have seen, remoter or more completely cut off from outside influences.

'For lust of knowing what should not be known', sang Flecker's pilgrims, 'we take the Golden Road to Samarkand.' Before the War, when I first went there, making my way across Siberia and down through Kazakstan, the whole of Russian Turkestan was still a forbidden zone from which all foreigners were rigorously excluded, and I only reached it after innumerable adventures. Today you simply book a seat on a Soviet jet airliner, which takes you in less than four hours from Moscow to Tashkent, capital of the Soviet Socialist Republic of Uzbekistan, and provides an adequate meal on the way. And from Tashkent it is only a short flight on to Samarkand.

From the airport you ride in across a wide dusty plain, dotted with ancient tombs and crumbling ruins. This is Afro Siab, called after a local king who lived centuries before Christ, and site of the ancient Maracanda. It was Maracanda that Alexander the Great stormed and sacked, and in Maracanda that in a fit of drunkenness he slew his friend Clitus, and, in addition to his other wives, wedded the beautiful Roxana, daughter of the

Sogdian general, Oxyartes. Through the centuries his name has gone down in Central Asia as the prophet-king Iskander d'Hulkarnein.

Then, topping a rise, you suddenly see the glittering domes and minarets of Samarkand spread out before you against a brilliant green background of gardens and trees. Though its history goes back to Alexander the Great and before, and though already in Marco Polo's day it was 'a very large and splendid city', Samarkand is above all the city of Tamerlane, who made it his capital and lies buried in the Gur Emir, under the splendid turquoise dome he built for his favourite grandson and himself more than five-and-a-half centuries ago.

Built and, as we have seen, immediately re-built in 1404, the last year of Tamerlane's life, the Gur Emir was originally part of a much larger complex containing a *khaniga* or guest-house, a medresseh, and several other buildings, all of which have long since disappeared. In addition to the tombs of Tamerlane and his grandson, Mohammed Sultan, the Gur Emir contains those of three of Tamerlane's sons, Omar Sheikh, Miranshah and Shakh Rukh, and of his grandson Ulug Beg, in whose reign it became the mausoleum of the Timurid dynasty. Also buried there, next to Tamerlane himself, is the famous sheikh Mir Sayed Barka.

Tamerlane's burial chamber is lined with jasper and alabaster, while his tombstone is made from a single slab of dark-green jade from China, bearing, one is told, the following inscription: 'He who opens this tomb will bring upon his country an invader more terrible than me.' In spite of this the tomb itself, which lies under a more modest marble stone in the crypt below the mosque, was opened more than thirty years ago by the famous Soviet archaeologist, Professor Gerasimov, and Tamerlane's skeleton taken out and examined. It showed him to have been a tall, powerful man with a straggling reddish moustache, and lame, as his name indicates, in one leg. But then, suddenly, so they say, on that June morning in 1941, as the good professor stood holding Tamerlane's skull in his hand and looking at it, one of his assistants burst into the crypt with news that left them thunderstruck, the news that a few hours earlier Hitler's armies had crossed the Soviet border.

In a corner of the courtyard of the Gur Emir lies *Kok Tash*, the Blue Stone, a long low block of bluish-grey marble carved with arabesques on the sides and once kept in the old citadel. This was the base of Timur's throne, and on it he and his successors were crowned. According to legend, it had, like other such stones, fallen from heaven and would not suffer a

Samarkand: at prayer

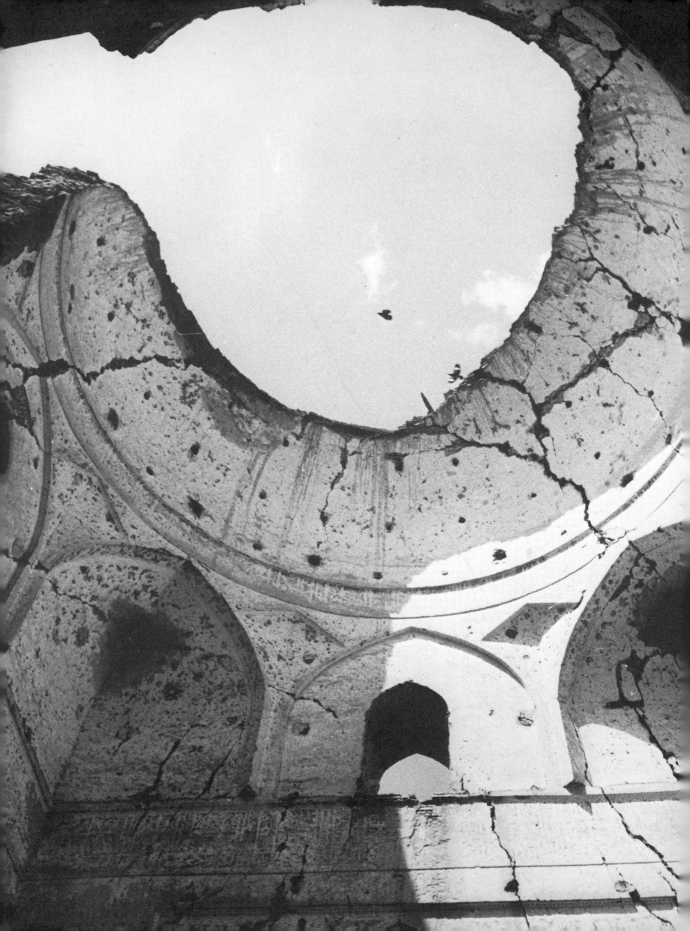

Samarkand: the Bibi Khanum

Samarkand: the
Shakh Zindeh

Samarkand: the Shakh Zindeh

Shakh Zindeh

Samarkand: the Mosque of Hodja Akhror

Samarkand: the Gur Emir

Samarkand: the Shir Dar

◀ Samarkand: the Shir Dar

In the Bazaar

Samarkand: the rice-seller

false Khan or one of dubious descent to approach it. Behind it is an object popularly supposed to be Timur's bath.

Not far from the Gur Emir stands the vast shattered arch of the great cathedral mosque of Bibi Khanum, also originally part of a larger complex and completed, like the Gur Emir, in the last frenzied year of Tamerlane's life. Bibi, so the story runs, was a Chinese, or possibly Mongolian, Princess who became Timur's wife and the mosque was built by a Persian architect who, while Tamerlane was away at the wars, fell in love with the Princess and imprinted on her cheek a kiss so passionate that it left a burn. Seeing this on his return, Tamerlane sent his men to kill the architect. But the Persian fled before them to the top of the highest minaret, and then, just as his pursuers were about to seize him, sprouted wings and, soaring high above Samarkand, flew back to his native town of Meshed.

In fact it seems probable that this is the mosque which Clavijo called 'the noblest of all we had seen in the city of Samarkand', and which he saw being re-built in the winter of 1404. On his return to Samarkand from India in 1399 Timur had given orders for the construction of a magnificent cathedral mosque to the memory of one of his mothers-in-law. Then he had gone campaigning again. In his absence master-craftsmen and masons had been brought to Samarkand from Bagdad and Basra, from Fars and Hindustan. Marble had come from Azerbaijan and crystal from Damascus. Slaves and teams of elephants working together had helped to build one of the biggest mosques in the world. Its great gates were made from an amalgam of seven metals. The huge Cufic lettering on its dome could be read from miles away. Its gigantic portal faced the medresseh of the Empress, Saray-Mulk-Khanum. By the time Timur came back from the wars, the great mosque was almost ready. But when he saw it, he did not like it. The portal, he said, was inadequate and must be pulled down and re-built. This, needless to say, was immediately done, while Tamerlane himself, as we have seen, personally supervised operations from his litter, urging on the workmen with coins and lumps of meat.

According to Ibn Arabshah, an admittedly hostile witness, the mosque was too hastily constructed and started to crumble almost before it was finished, so that the faithful were reluctant to worship in it for fear of stones falling from the roof. Today, certainly, it is in ruins, though this may be partly due to earthquakes and to the hazards of war. We know that in the nineteenth century it served as a cotton market and was also used by the Russian soldiers for stabling their horses, while its once-famous gates were melted down and used for making coins by an avaricious Emir of Bokhara. A little distance away stands a great marble lectern for the Koran, originally placed in the mosque by Ulug Beg and later moved outside when the structure began to crumble.

Tamerlane made Samarkand the most splendid city of its time, and to this day you can still see the remains of its magnificence. In the middle of the Old City is the cobbled expanse of the Registan, which Lord Curzon, who went there in the eighteen-eighties, a dozen years after its capture by the Russians, called 'the noblest public square in the world'. It is enclosed on three sides by three ancient medressehs with their fluted domes, their minarets, their great arches and their spacious courtyards. These are now being carefully and skilfully restored, and on a recent visit I watched with interest the processes by which the restorers were managing to produce glazed tiles identical to those used in the time of Tamerlane.

On the northern side of the Registan stands the Tilla Kari or Golden Mosque Medresseh, built in the middle of the seventeenth century and called after the great mosque which forms part of it. On the western side, to your left as you face the square, is the smaller but older and more beautiful medresseh of Ulug Beg the astronomer, Tamerlane's grandson. Ulug Beg built it in 1417. He also built a remarkable observatory which can still be seen on the outskirts of the city, with its vast stone quadrant and other instruments still in position. Today, in Soviet Uzbekistan, Ulug Beg is well thought of, as having done his best to represent science and enlightenment against the forces of reaction and obscurantism, which, it is said, were responsible, together with his less enlightened son Abd al-Latif, for his early and violent demise. He lies buried, near his grandfather, in the Gur Emir. To your right, on the eastern side of the Registan, opposite the medresseh of Ulug Beg, and built to balance it, is Shir Dar, the Lion Bearer, put up in the first half of the seventeenth century by Yallangtush, who also built the Tilla Kari. Across the top of the great central arch sprawls the splendid yellow lion or possibly tiger that gives it its name. On either side of the façade rise beautifully proportioned twin domes of dazzling blue. Behind the façades of the three medressehs lie enclosed courtyards, onto which open what were once the cells of the religious teachers and their pupils.

Before the rise of Islam, Samarkand had for a time been a Christian See, and Marco Polo has a story that under the Mongols, in Chaghatai's day, the Christians of Samarkand, encouraged by Chaghatai's reported conversion to their faith, built a great church there in honour of St John the Baptist. As a base for the central column which supported the roof, they took 'a very beautiful stone belonging to the Saracens'. This the Saracens not unnaturally resented, and after Chaghatai's death demanded it back. The Christians, explaining that to remove the stone would destroy their church, offered them gold and treasure in its place. But to no avail: the Saracens wanted the stone, and Chaghatai's successor gave the Christians two days in which to produce it. 'The Christians', Marco tells us, were 'greatly perplexed and did not know what to do.' But 'when morning came on the day on which the stone was to be handed over, the column that rested on the stone rose up ... to a height of fully three palms and stayed there as firmly supported as if the stone had remained in this position'. 'And', adds Marco conclusively, 'there it still is. And this was, and still is, accounted one of the greatest miracles that have happened in the world.'

The Church of St John with its miraculous column suspended in mid-air has long since disappeared, and the great mosques and medressehs of the Registan are today no longer places of worship. But a mile or two away in the suburbs of the old town the traveller can still find a smaller and more modest shrine which in the eyes of the faithful has retained all its sanctity, the Mosque of Hodja Akhror, built in the early seventeenth century by an uncle of the reigning Emir and called after the fifteenth-century saint of that name who lies buried there and who, it appears, was celebrated not only for his holiness but also for his immense wealth. Here, in the dappled shade of the ancient plane trees which surround the tranquil waters of the central pool, devout Moslems still come to pray, and here you may see robed and turbaned figures kneeling absorbed in prayer or silently prostrating themselves in the direction of Mecca. The tomb of the saint lies outside the main enclosure, with lesser monuments clustered about it. It is hard to imagine a more peaceful refuge from the bustle and turmoil of the world.

Beyond the city to the north cluster the cupolas of a superb avenue of ancient tombs built up the side of a hill on both sides of a narrow passage-way, Hazreti Shakh Zindeh, the Shrine of the Living King. Kasim Ibn Abbas, the Living King, was, it seems, a cousin of the Prophet Mohammed, who converted Soghdiana to Islam in the seventh century at the time of the Arab invasions and was later hunted down and decapitated by the local Nestorian Christians, or, according to another account, saved from his pursuers when a rock opened miraculously before him and swallowed him up. The building of the shrine was begun in 1326, after the Mongol conquest, and continued under Tamerlane and Ulug Beg. But there is evidence that it was already a place of pilgrimage long before that.

Entering the great gate at the foot of the hill, which was built by Ulug Beg, you first climb a steep flight of stairs. Above you to the left rises the fine blue-domed tomb of (one is told) Timur's nurse. At the head of the stairs stands a white arch, and beyond this a paved alley-way leads between the tiled façades of two lines of miniature mosques to yet another arched gateway. Immediately on the left rise the two plain turquoise domes of the Mausoleum of Kazi Zadeh Rumi, a great astronomer from Turkey who was Ulug Beg's teacher, and the tombs of one of Timur's sons and of his first wife, Turkan. The interior of the Turkan Aka, which is covered with intricate designs in mosaic, is particularly fine and contains a number of ancient tombstones besides that of Turkan herself. On the right, across the alley-way, are the tombs of the Emir Hussein, of one of Timur's sisters, and of one of his daughters. Also buried nearby is Shady Mulik, Tamerlane's favourite niece, who died in 1371, when she was twenty-four and he himself only thirty-five. But clearly much of this is no more than intelligent guesswork on the part of the experts.

By the side of the gate, at the far end of the alley-way, grow two ancient trees. According to legend, Kasim Ibn Abbas, hard pressed by his Christian pursuers and seeing that his horse was at its last gasp, threw away his riding whip, which, on touching the ground, struck roots and eventually grew into these two trees. Cuttings from them, it is said, will cure all known diseases.

Passing through the arch at the end of the alley-way, you emerge into a beautiful small courtyard surrounded by more handsome tiled buildings. Facing each other across it are the shrines of Kutluk and Nuir, built in memory of another of Timur's wives and one of his daughters, that of Kutluk being ornamented with dazzling turquoise pillars carved in high relief. Opposite you now is the early fourteenth-century shrine of Hodja Ahmed, and, passing through a pair of fine doors of fretted wood and along a dark passage, you finally reach the magnificently decorated mosque and octagonal mausoleum of the Living King, both built in 1334-5. Here you will be shown the fine blue-tiled tombstone under which Kasim's mortal remains are said to be buried. But those who know better will tell you that Kasim is in fact still living, and lurks nearby in a disused cistern, where for thirteen centuries he has been waiting, with his severed head beneath his arm, for the moment to emerge and claim the kingdom that awaits him.

Today, as in Tamerlane's day, the real centre of life in Samarkand, as in any city of Central Asia, is the bazaar. This lies across the way from the Registan, not far away from the single dome which is all that is left of the old covered bazaar. Here people not only buy and sell, but meet their friends and hear the latest gossip. Half a century after the Revolution, the keen commercial instincts of the inhabitants still survive. Anywhere else, a foreigner at once becomes the centre of attention; here Mohammed himself, or, for that matter, Karl Marx, might walk past unnoticed, so absorbed is everyone by the business of buying and selling. 'Posht!' cry the donkeymen irritably, as they push their way through the dense crowds.

Not far from the bazaar, under the shade of some ancient trees, is the main *chai-khana* or tea-house of the city, where everyone forgathers to sit cross-legged and talk and drink the famous green tea of Central Asia. This fragrant beverage is brought to one in graceful porcelain teapots from which one pours it into fragile-looking little bowls. Slightly bitter in taste, it is remarkably refreshing and has a surprisingly stimulating effect on the intellect. The people of Samarkand and indeed of all Central Asia consume it in enormous quantities.

9 *Bokhara the Noble*

An hour's flight westwards from Samarkand, or some eight hours by bus or by train, along the fertile valley of the Zeravshan, lies Bokhara. Once the holiest city in all Central Asia, boasting over 350 mosques and over 100 religious colleges, it was formerly known as *Bokhara es Sherif*, Bokhara the Noble. Marco Polo, writing in the thirteenth century, speaks of it as '*une cité moult noble et grant*', the finest in all Persia, and three hundred years later Anthony Jenkinson tells us of its 'high walls of earth and its many houses, temples and monuments of stone sumptuously builded and gilt'.

When I first saw Bokhara in 1938, it was still a completely eastern walled city of enclosed mud-built houses, each looking inwards on its own courtyard. At that time only very few Western Europeans had ever set eyes on it. Today a big boulevard has been driven through the centre of it, and it is well on the way to becoming an ordinary Soviet city. But Bokhara, for all that, still retains many reminders of a prodigious and bloodstained past.

Above the dusty expanse of the Registan rises the thousand-year-old bulk of the Citadel or Ark, containing within its fortifications a veritable rabbit-warren of tumbledown palaces, mosques, harems and offices. Much of it was destroyed when the last Emir set fire to it as he fled in the summer of 1920 before the rapidly advancing Red Cavalry, and you may still see in his study the antiquated telephone which warned him of their approach. The great entrance gate is flanked by twin turrets, between which, at the time of my first visit, still hung the clock made for the Emir in about 1840 by an Italian watchmaker, Giovanni Orlandi of Parma, who was eventually bludgeoned to death for refusing to become a Mohammedan or, some say, for allowing the Emir's watch to stop.

You enter the Ark by a steep, dark, winding passage-way flanked on either side by sinister-looking guardrooms and torture chambers and cells for prisoners. This was the way taken on his arrival in Bokhara on 27 April 1844 by Dr Joseph Wolff, curate of the parish of High Hoyland in Yorkshire, wearing, in his own words, 'full canonicals: clergyman's gown, doctor's hood and shovel hat' and carrying a Bible under his arm, while the population gathered in their thousands to stare at him.

By origin the son of a Bavarian rabbi, by vocation (after a brief but lively encounter with Rome) a clergyman of the Church of England, Dr Wolff was known to his contemporaries, and not without reason, as the Eccentric Missionary.

After an early life spent travelling to a number of improbable places, Dr Wolff had set out from London in October 1843 at the age of nearly fifty on what was to be the most famous of all his journeys. His purpose was to find out what had happened to two British officers, friends of his, Colonel Stoddart and Captain Conolly. Stoddart and Conolly had been sent some time before on a rather ill-defined mission to the court of the Emir Nasrullah, the bloodthirsty ruffian who was at that time ruling over Bokhara. Their object was to induce him to place his dominions under British rather than under Russian protection, for the British Government were by now seriously alarmed at the way in which the Russians were reaching out into Central Asia.

Bokhara in those days was almost completely cut off from the outside world, and it was a long time before any news of the two officers reached London. When news did come, it was vague and disturbing. According to some accounts, they had been thrown into jail. According to others, they had been done to death. No one knew for certain what had happened to them.

It is at this stage that Dr Wolff makes his appearance, wearing the red and black gown of a Doctor of Divinity, with a shovel hat on his head and a Bible under his arm, riding alone, for his servants had deserted him, and rather awkwardly, for he was an extremely poor horseman. His journey across waterless desert infested with marauding tribes had been hazardous in the extreme. But he had finally reached his destination. It now only remained for him to find out what had happened to Stoddart and Conolly.

He was to find this out soon enough. After long months of imprisonment the two envoys had finally been consigned to a well, twenty-one feet deep, in which the Emir kept a selection of specially bred vermin and reptiles. When, two months later, 'after masses of their flesh had been gnawed off their bones', they still refused to turn Mohammedan, they had been taken out and beheaded in front of the citadel.

Dr Wolff had not been in Bokhara long when the question of his own religious proclivities was raised, and the Chief Executioner sent, perhaps a little pointedly, to ask whether or not he was prepared to embrace Islam.

Wolff's reply to this inquiry was short and to the point. 'Decidedly not', he said, and then — for there could be no doubt what the alternative would be — he sat down to write a farewell letter to his wife, Lady Georgina, whom he had left at home in Yorkshire.

But Wolff's life, as it turned out, was saved by the strangeness of his appearance and behaviour. On his being brought before the Emir, still clad in full canonicals and with his Bible still under his arm, that potentate was seized with a fit of uncontrollable laughter, which redoubled when, instead of the prescribed three, the Eccentric Missionary prostrated himself thirty times, stroked his beard thirty times and cried *Allah Akbar*, God is Great, thirty times. For, though not prepared to become a Mohammedan, Dr Wolff was understandably ready to go to considerable lengths in order to keep out of the vermin pit. The interview was thus a distinct success and culminated with the appearance of a 'musical band of Hindoos from Lahore' who gave a spirited rendering of a tune which he quickly identified as 'God Save the Queen'.

After further adventures, which included his temptation by means of an unveiled woman, specially sent for this purpose by the Emir's Prime Minister, Dr Wolff was eventually allowed to leave Bokhara alive, greatly to the surprise of the population, who were unaccustomed to any such act of clemency on the part of their ruler.

Making your way up through the narrow entrance passage and into the Ark itself, you come to the courtyard where the Emir had his throne and where Colonel Stoddart, wearing his cocked hat and his sword, refused to bow down to him, striking out angrily at the court official who tried to make him do so. And just behind the Ark is the Zindan, the prison with the vermin pit in which Nasrullah kept his victims. Today, under the Soviet Government, the pit is displayed as a monument to the depravity of oriental potentates. At the bottom crouch two battered but lifelike dummies, while a villainous-looking jailer in Bokharan uniform gazes vindictively down on them from above. To this day the names of Stoddart and Conolly, or *Khan Ali*, as they called him, are still remembered in Bokhara.

Not far from the Ark rises *Kok Gumbaz*, the turquoise-blue dome of the great Kalyan Mosque, re-built in the fifteenth century by the Shaibanid khans on the site of an earlier cathedral mosque. Here the Emir used to worship in person, and here Stoddart for a time was forced to worship

Bokhara: two Uzbeks

Bokhara: in the Registan

In conversation

Old Bokhara

Bokhara   The Storyteller   The flower-sellers ▶

A craftsman

Bokhara The brothers

The engraver

Bokhara: 'Lenin is always with us'

Bokhara

with him. High above it and above all Bokhara looms menacingly the elaborately decorated twelfth-century Kalyan Minaret, or Tower of Death, as it is called, from the top of which, under the Emirs, on bazaar days, condemned criminals used to be thrown down to their destruction. 'Like large parcels' wrote Monsieur Moser, a nineteenth-century French travel-ler, who from his window, 'by way of distraction', observed their descent, twisting and turning in mid air as they fell. With time, it appears, the re-peated impact of these terrible packages produced a little hollow in the hard ground at the foot of the minaret.

Of the hundreds of other mosques and medressehs which Bokhara once boasted a fair number still survive. Opposite the main entrance of the Masjid-i Kalyan, and as it were balancing it, stands the rather smaller medresseh of Mir-i Arab, built in 1535 by Sheikh Mir-i Arab for the ruler of the day, Ubaydullah Khan, with the proceeds of the successful sale into slavery of several thousand Persian Shiahs who were unlucky enough to fall into his hands. Today both monarch and builder lie buried in one of the rooms of the medresseh. This is still in use as a religious college, and on a recent visit I had a long and rewarding interview with the director of studies, a brisk young man in a smart blue suit, who, it occurred to me, might possibly double the role with that of political commissar.

To the south-west of the Registan are the Kosh Medresseh, or twinned medressehs of Abdullah Khan, built in 1588, and of Madar-i Khan, literally the Khan's mother, built in memory of Abdullah's mother a score of years earlier. Both belong to a period of mediocre artistic achievement and neither attains a very high standard either architecturally or in its ornamentation.

Like those in Samarkand, the mosques and medressehs of Bokhara are constructed of sun-baked bricks. The design is usually the same: in the centre of the façade the central arch, or *pishtak*, reaching the whole height of the building, with, on either side, a double row of smaller arches. In the medressehs the central arch forms the entrance to one or more courtyards surrounded by cloisters and rows of cells in which seminarists and pilgrims and visiting divines once had their being and pursued their studies. Only the Mir-i Arab is still usèd as a religious college.

Most of the mosques in Bokhara have lost the coloured tiles which once adorned them; but one pair of medressehs, those of Ulug Beg and Abd al-Aziz, which stand facing each other across a narrow lane not far from the Tower of Death, have retained at least some of their former splendour, their façades being still decorated with their original intricate arabesques. The Ulug Beg medresseh, like the medresseh of the same name in Samarkand, was built by Ulug Beg in the early fifteenth century, the medresseh of Abd al-Aziz more than two centuries later. Of the two, though the later building is larger and more elaborate, the earlier has greater purity and harmony of style and decoration.

A few of the lesser mosques are still in use; but for the most part they stand abandoned or have been turned to other uses. Of the buildings which stand round the Liabi Khaus, the tree-shaded pool in the centre of the town, the seventeenth-century Nadir Divan Begi *khaniga*, or guest-house, is now a much-frequented billiard club, and the adjoining Nadir Divan Begi medresseh a hotel, while the local public record office is housed in the 160 cells of the sixteenth-century Kukeldash medresseh. As for the Liabi Khaus itself, it echoes with shouts and splashes, as dozens of little Uzbek boys take headers into its turgid waters, while their elders sip their green tea and take their ease under the trees of the neighbouring *chai-khana*.

Water is carried through Bokhara by a series of open channels, linked with the Liabi Khaus and other pools and ultimately via the Shakh Rud, the Royal Canal, with the Zerafshan. In less enlightened times, in fact until quite recently, these were used indiscriminately by the inhabitants for washing and drinking as well as for a number of other less salubrious purposes, with the result that a peculiarly unattractive type of tapeworm, causing suppurating boils, and various other unpleasant water-borne parasites and diseases, were more or less endemic. 'The water thereof is most unholsome', writes Anthony Jenkinson. Now all through the town warning posters impress on the inhabitants of Bokhara the paramount importance of personal hygiene.

Some distance away from the centre of Bokhara through a maze of mud-baked houses is a most unusual building of a much later period, the Char Minar, or Four Minarets. This strange little structure with four bulbous minarets, each with its stork's nest, dwarfing a low central dome, was originally built in 1807 by a rich Bokharan merchant as the gate-house to a medresseh which has since disappeared. Near the Tower of Death are the baths and the covered bazaars, once the richest in Central Asia. Now, only clusters of beehive-shaped domes are left at the point where two or more streets intersect and, where rubies and emeralds once changed hands, a desultory trade is carried on in ice cream and fizzy drinks. Yet another survival from the Middle Ages are the caravanserais, where the caravans arriving in Bokhara from the outside world once made halt. Today teeming families of Bokharans live in them, sleeping in the surrounding cells and overflowing in the daytime into the central courtyards. On top of almost every building in Bokhara is perched a stork's nest each summer, and the air resounds with the clicking of their beaks. When I first visited Bokhara in 1938, its walls and battlements and eleven gates and watch-towers were still standing in all their crumbling magnificence. Today this is no longer so. Most of the walls have been demolished, to let in the air, one is told. But here and there enough of them remains to give you some idea of what they once were like.

Outside the city, on some waste land beyond the newly laid out Park of Rest and Culture, not far from what is left of the walls, are two buildings of great antiquity, at least one of which belongs to the pre-Mongol period: the Shrine of Chasma Ayub and the Mausoleum of Ismael Samani. Chasma Ayub, or Job's Spring, is supposed to have been built by Tamerlane on the site of a miraculous spring which gushed forth there at the behest of the Prophet Job, but in style it belongs to a much earlier period. The Mausoleum of Ismael Samani, a strange-looking little building decorated with elaborate small floral designs in fired brick, was built for himself by the founder of the Samanid dynasty in the ninth century A.D. To bind the mortar he used, they say, camel's milk and white of egg, and they have certainly done their task well through the centuries. Of particular interest is its small dome set on a cubiform drum, a new architectural principle which was to be made use of in Central Asia for the next five centuries. Nearby, unimpressed by their historic surroundings, a whole swarm of little Uzbek boys perched like birds in a tree as I passed, and called out to have their picture taken, while a little further on a young mother rocked her swaddled baby in an ancient cradle as his little brother stood proudly by.

Bokhara has always been famous for its craftsmanship, and in its workshops caps and waistcoats are still embroidered in gold thread, and brass and silver vessels engraved with traditional ornaments and patterns which have been handed down through the centuries. In a courtyard at the end of a winding dusty lane I watched a very old man in a white turban drawing out the designs for these with immense care, while the hammering of the metal-workers echoed all round him. By his side stood the usual pot of refreshing green tea.

In Bokhara, as in Samarkand, the inhabitants, both the townspeople

and, to an even greater extent, the peasants who come in from the surrounding country, have kept their national dress and way of life. In the
bazaar, in the tea-houses, and on Fridays in the mosques, you may still see
the men wearing their traditional turbans and brightly striped robes. For
women, the veil has now gone out, though fifteen or twenty years ago you
could still occasionally catch a glimpse of a completely veiled woman,
covered from top to toe by a *paranja*, a black horsehair screen rather like a
meat-safe, and even now many older women still keep their faces half
covered from inquisitive eyes.

10 *The Old Order Changeth*

Once or twice recently, after driving up into the mountains to the south of Samarkand, near the village of Urgut, three or four thousand feet above the plain, I have eaten my midday meal with some Uzbek friends under a gigantic sycamore by a clear pool in which we all bathed. Nearby is a sacred grove of giant sycamores, dating back seven or eight hundred years, to long before the days of Tamerlane or Jenghiz Khan. This for Moslems is a place of particular holiness, and, as we sat there, passing wayfarers would continually stop to pray by its limpid waters. At one end was a great stone ring with a stream pouring through it. Any woman who swam through it, we were told, was bound to produce any number of children. A girl in our party was pushed through repeatedly, with what subsequent result I have been unable to ascertain.

Peaceful as it now seems, Urgut as lately as the nineteen-twenties was a robber stronghold. After the Revolution the Soviet Government had a problem on their hands in Turkestan. Resistance to the new regime was rife and was vigorously fanned by the mullahs. In the summer of 1920, after nearly three years of uneasy co-existence with his Bolshevik neighbours, the last Emir of Bokhara, Abdul Said Mir Alim Khan, had at length been dethroned and had fled headlong to the mountains, dropping favourite dancing-boy after favourite dancing-boy in his wake, in the hope of thus delaying the Red Cavalry, to whom, rightly or wrongly, he attributed his own deplorable tastes. But for some years after this isolated groups of basmachis or banditti carried on the fight in the mountains, and in 1922 the former Turkish War Minister Enver Pasha, who dreamed of founding a pan-Turanian Empire stretching from Stamboul to Shanghai, was still able to rally substantial support for a last stand against the rising tide of Bolshevism.

Leaving Turkey after his country's defeat in 1918, Enver had made his way first to Germany and thence to Moscow. There, in the autumn of 1921, he somehow persuaded Lenin to entrust him with the task of pacifying Turkestan, where the scale of the insurrection and the numbers of new

93

recruits now joining the basmachis were becoming a source of ever greater concern to the Soviet authorities. Enver, who had other, personal, plans for Turkestan, reached Bokhara on 8 November 1921. Three days later he left again, ostensibly on a shooting expedition. Shortly afterwards the Soviet authorities were distressed to learn that he had in fact himself joined the basmachis near Shirabad in the hill country of eastern Bokhara.

A few years earlier, during the First World War, Enver had led an entire Turkish Army to disaster on the Caucasus front. As a leader of irregulars he was more successful. Soon he had built up in the mountains an effective guerrilla force controlled by an efficient general staff, and arms, money and supplies were reaching him from a number of different sources, including the former Emir of Bokhara, who from exile in Afghanistan now appointed him Commander-in-Chief of his armed forces.

But Enver had wider ambitions. From his headquarters in the mountains of eastern Bokhara he now issued a proclamation announcing the formation of a new independent Moslem State in Central Asia. At the same time he re-established the Caliphate and proclaimed himself Emir of Turkestan. A special golden seal prepared for use on official documents described him as Commander-in-Chief of all the Armies of Islam, Son-in-Law of the Caliph, and Representative of the Prophet.

The strongly Moslem character of Enver's regime further enhanced his popularity with the mullahs, whose influence everywhere was still very strong, while his personal prestige and leadership, the disturbed state of the country, and the widespread dislike of the Soviet regime and of the Russians as such, all contributed to his success. His first victory was a daring raid on the city of Bokhara itself. After inflicting heavy casualties on the enemy and doing much damage, he again withdrew to the hills. From now onwards each defeat inflicted on the Red Army brought him in more volunteers, more arms and more supplies. Some of those who joined him were basmachis, others former members of the Emir's forces, and others deserters from the Red Army. Soon a large part of the territory of Bokhara was in the hands of the insurgents.

By the spring of 1922 the situation had become deeply disturbing for the Bolsheviks. Their troops, mostly European Russians, were at a serious disadvantage. In wild, unfamiliar mountainous country, suffering from heat, from lack of food and water, from dysentery and malaria, surrounded by a hostile native population, harassed by surprise attacks, unable to move without fear of ambush, they were obliged to contend with a mobile, well-led, well-equipped enemy, knowing every inch of the country and enjoying the support of its inhabitants. But, for all this, when in May 1922 the Moscow Government received from their former protégé, Enver, writing as Supreme Commander of the Armies of Bokhara, Khiva and Turkestan, a letter offering peace and friendship in return for diplomatic recognition and the withdrawal of their troops, they rejected it out of hand and started preparations to crush the rebellion once and for all.

Enver, meanwhile, like other leaders of irregular troops, was not finding it easy to preserve unity in his own forces, and more than one of the basmachi leaders, who had at first supported him, began to show signs of turning against him. Having rejected his offer of peace, the Russians now despatched strong reinforcements to Turkestan and launched an all-out offensive against his positions in the hills. Soon things began to go badly for Enver. Many of the hill tribes abandoned him or turned against him. While the Russians advanced from the direction of Husar, one former basmachi leader pressed forward from Sharshan in the north, and another attacked him treacherously from Shirabad in the south. Having shifted his headquarters to the village of Kafirnigan, he was suddenly attacked by two regiments of Red Cavalry, who took him by surprise and forced him to fly headlong, leaving everything behind him.

But Enver Pasha did not despair. Moving to the gorges of the Yurchi, he again took the offensive, raiding the Red Army's camel-trains and playing havoc with their lines of communication. Every time the enemy sought to pin him down, he would slip through their fingers and strike again where they least expected it. Though the forces under his command were scattered and diminished and he himself a fugitive in the mountains, he still in a sense retained the initiative and still remained a serious menace to the Soviet position in Central Asia.

For the Red Army, the big problem by the end of July 1922 was to find Enver. So long as he remained alive, neither the High Command of the Red Army in Turkestan nor, for that matter, their masters in Moscow could enjoy a moment's peace. The question was to discover where, in all that wild tangle of mountain ranges, he was lurking, and how to pin him down and bring him to battle.

In the end intelligence was received that Enver's headquarters were in a certain hamlet in the area of Dennau, and a force of Red Cavalry was sent to surround and attack him. The troops closed in, and at five o'clock on the morning of 4 August 1922, having first dispersed his force so as to cut off his enemy's possible lines of withdrawal, the Red Commander gave orders for the attack on the village to begin. The basmachis were not entirely taken by surprise. Their sentries gave the alarm and a fierce battle developed. In the end, finding his retreat cut off, many of his troops gone, and the remainder heavily outnumbered by the enemy, Enver decided to die gloriously. Mounting his horse, he charged straight at the oncoming enemy.

When the Bolsheviks later came to examine the enemy dead, they found among all the bodies dressed in turbans and khalats one that was clad in breeches and boots and a tightly buttoned tunic. The head had been completely severed from the body by a tremendous sabre-cut. On one finger was a valuable signet ring. Some papers in a pocket showed the dead man to be Enver Pasha. Near him lay a miniature Koran which he had been holding in his hand as he charged, and which, with his papers, eventually found its way into the archives of the Soviet Secret Police.*

For ten or fifteen years after Enver's death little news came out of Soviet Central Asia. In the early years after the Revolution, Stalin was put in charge of the 'problem of the nationalities'. Before long he was in charge of everything else as well. 'Imagine Jenghiz Khan with a telephone', Leo Tolstoi had said with considerable prescience not so many years before. From time to time it was officially announced that this or that holder of high office in the government or party had been tried and executed on charges of 'bourgeois nationalism', and in March 1938 I saw Faisullah Khodjayev, until his arrest some months earlier President of Uzbekistan and one of the foremost Central Asian revolutionary leaders, condemned to death before a military court in Moscow as a traitor and a 'bourgeois nationalist'. But, whatever truth there may have been in these charges at the time, there are today precious few signs of nationalism, let alone separatism, in Soviet Turkestan.

Mohammedanism and the Mohammedan way of life die hard. Though in subdued and modified form, the Mohammedan religion still survives in Turkestan. On Fridays the surviving mosques are crowded and, as the high wailing cry of the muezzin sounds from the minaret, you may see a great concourse of dedicated worshippers bowing down and standing up and intoning the responses and prayers, while afterwards alms and gifts of food are distributed to the deserving poor. Even those shrines which have officially been deconsecrated and turned into museums still receive a steady

*Another version of Enver's end is given in the present author's *A Person from England* (p. 358).

Bokhara: the Tower of Death

Bokhara   The Ark
                The Ark: the Empty Throne

Bokhara: Liabi Khavs and the medresseh of Nadir Divan Begi

Bokhara
The Registan

A street near a town

In the Chai Khana

Bokhara   The Mir Arab medresseh

The medresseh of Abdul Aziz Khan ▶

Bokhara   A city gate

The city walls

Bokhara: the janitor of the medresseh

Bokhara   The Covered Bazaar

A vegetable-seller

Inside the Covered Bazaar ▶

Bokhara   At prayer

In the Mosque

Alms

Bokhara   The Kalyan Mosque and Kok Gumbaz

The Char Minar ▶

The donkey park

Bokhara   The Mausoleum of Ismael Samani

Chasma Ayub

stream of visitors whose interest is clearly religious rather than cultural, and in Samarkand, as you climb from one blue-domed tomb of the Shakh-i-Zindeh to another, you find that, despite the crude, rather half-hearted Anti-God Museum which has been installed at the entrance, you are constantly breaking in on the meditations of devout Mohammedans who have come with their families to visit the shrines and pray.

But those in authority are not seriously concerned. The problem is no longer acute. Forty or fifty years ago the Soviet authorities were still having trouble with the mullahs. Now there are few, if any, signs of conflict. Islam today is no longer a menace, scarcely even a nuisance to the Soviet Government. Indeed there are even signs that it might from their point of view have actual advantages as an instrument of policy in the Middle East, and Soviet Moslems are allowed, indeed encouraged, to keep in touch with Moslems in other countries.

Some years back, I had dinner in Tashkent with Ziyuddin Khan Ibn Mufti Khan Babakhan, the present Grand Mufti of Central Asia, and a venerable group of Imams from neighbouring mosques. From what Ziyuddin Khan told me, in the course of an agreeable meal served in a high, airy, whitewashed room adorned with bright green tiles bearing texts from the Koran, it appeared that his relations with the Soviet authorities were perfectly correct. He did not receive financial help from them; for that he depended on voluntary contributions from the Moslem population. But they showed themselves reasonably co-operative, provided facilities for the restoration and maintenance of mosques, and some years ago had enabled him to print an edition of the Koran for the first time since the Revolution. The number of practising Mohammedans, he claimed, was on the increase, more mosques were open, and a number of young men were being trained up as mullahs, some in Tashkent and others in Bokhara. He was able to keep in touch with Mohammedans in other countries, and of late had welcomed many Moslem visitors from abroad. As I signed my name in the visitors' book, I noted that President Nasser of Egypt had been there not long before.

Meanwhile, throughout Central Asia the process of modernization and Sovietization is proceeding apace. Wherever you go, you will find the old order making way for the new: ancient customs and traditions disappearing and new, up-to-date Soviet ones taking their place; new buildings going up and a new, more efficient, more hygienic, but from the sightseer's point of view far less picturesque, way of life being established.

This is particularly true of Tashkent. Once the capital of the Province of Turkestan and the seat of the Tsar's Governor-General, it is now capital of the Republic of Uzbekistan, and, with a population of a million and a quarter, has kept its position as the chief city of Central Asia and the focus of a flourishing cotton industry. When I first knew it, it was still neatly divided into a European city and an Uzbek one — rather like a garrison town in British India — with the cantonments of the conquering race arranged in well-laid-out avenues, and the native quarter clustering round the bazaar. What is left of the old native town is now fast disappearing. Part has already been replaced by new parks and avenues and blocks of flats and well-stocked department stores, and by an immense stadium, and more is being demolished and rebuilt every day: so much so that each time one goes back there, it is harder than ever to find one's bearings. This process has been further accelerated by the earthquake of 1966, after which an immense re-building programme was enthusiastically pushed through with the help of special teams of builders from all over the Soviet Union.

Only after a long walk did I eventually find what remained of the old town. Donkeys drifted down dusty lanes. Through doorways in high windowless walls of sun-baked brick one caught intimate glimpses of family life in tree-shaded courtyards. Attracted by sounds of uproar and music, I looked into one of these to find a wedding in progress. 'Come in! Come in!' they said. 'Be our guest.' And in a matter of minutes I had been introduced to the bride and bridegroom and their four grandfathers and a large number of other people, and was sitting cross-legged on the floor eating (with my fingers) mutton *plov* and grapes and jam and chocolates and sour cream, and drinking cup after cup of green tea, while the musicians played louder and louder on their weird instruments. All around were the wedding presents, including two television sets, both going at full blast, and numerous shiny teapots and samovars. The very young bride and bridegroom were both Uzbeks. (It is unusual for an Uzbek girl to marry a Russian, though Uzbek men sometimes marry Russian girls.) They and their scores of friends (including several Russians) seemed genuinely delighted to see an unexplained foreigner, and the bride at once presented me with her little bouquet. When I left, several hours later, full of food and green tea, half a dozen of the party insisted on escorting me home along the banks of the canal and through the darkening streets.

Comparing the two ways of life, the old and the new, the dirty, cosy village life of the little sun-baked mud houses and cool tree-shaded lanes and courtyards, and the orderly, stereotyped, hygienic existence of the soaring blocks of tenements, with their thousands of identical flats on hundreds of identical stairways and their zealous, watchful party members on each and every stairway, I could not help reflecting that from Moscow's point of view the advantages of this change were not only social; they were also in a high degree political and ideological as well.

11 *Khiva*

But the ultimate in hygienic modernization I was to find in the remote oasis of Khiva, once Khorezm, hundreds of miles away across the desert to the north-west, on the banks of the River Oxus, where it was first established, so the story goes, by Sim, the son of Noah. This I had finally succeeded in reaching in 1967 after innumerable unsuccessful attempts, only to discover that I was too late to see Khiva as it once had been. Here, where the Khans of Khiva and before them the Khorezmshahs had their capital, the inhabitants have now been moved out and housed elsewhere in modern apartment houses, while the town itself, complete and as it stands with its mosques and minarets, its palaces, bazaars and baths, is being converted into one great museum for the benefit of any tourists who may some day manage to get there. To the powers that be, the very idea of one of the former inhabitants drifting back to revisit his old home is obnoxious, and those you see about the streets have a furtive, hunted look. 'Go away, old man. *Go away*', said my companion irritably to an elderly Khivan whom we met unexpectedly round a street corner, and I barely had time to lift my camera before he was gone.

For all that, one has to admit that Ichan Kala, the walled and fortified Inner City of Khiva, though empty, presents an amazingly complete picture of a Central Asian city precinct, with its fortresses, its walls and gates, its caravanserai and covered bazaar, its mosques and palace and baths and ordinary dwelling-houses, all still standing exactly as they were in the days of the last Khan. Nothing is missing except the inhabitants.

All round the Inner City its walls, built partly of clay and partly of sun-baked bricks, are still standing, with their ramparts, bastions and gates. Oblong in shape, the Ichan Kala lies roughly north and south. Approaching it from the west and entering by Ata Darvaza, the West Gate, you come immediately upon Kunya Ark, the Old Ark or Citadel, which until the early nineteenth century also served as the residence and seat of government of the Khans. A fortress within a fortress, its walls enclose a man-made mound. This is crowned with the crumbling ruins of a castle, bearing the intriguing name of Akshikh-Bobo. From it you look out across the gardens, mulberry trees, orchards and vineyards of Dishan Kala, the Outer City, to the irrigated fields beyond them, and then, quite suddenly, to the howling wilderness of the Kara Kum.

In spite of its name, the Old Citadel only dates back to the seventeenth century. Of the complex of courtyards and buildings where the Khans once held court, took council and dispensed justice, much has now disappeared, but from the ruins of the castle you look down on the aivans or pillared recesses of the mosque built by Allah Kuli Khan (1825–42) and of the older Kurinishkhana. In this context it is interesting to find, when one gets to Khiva, that most of the buildings there, though not dissimilar in style from those of Samarkand or Bokhara, are by contrast of quite recent origin, dating in the main from the first half of the nineteenth century, when a remarkable late flowering of Islamic art and architecture seems to have taken place, possibly induced by the arrival in the oasis of numbers of skilled craftsmen and artisans from Persia.

Opposite the entrance to the Ark is a large and ornate mosque and medresseh built in 1871 by Mohammed Rahim Khan II (1865–1910) and bearing his name. But far more striking are the neighbouring mosque, medresseh and minaret of Madamin, or Mohammed Amin Khan. These stand immediately to the south of the Old Citadel and were built in 1851–2. It was the intention of Madamin Khan that they should outshine every other building in Khiva and that their minaret should be the tallest in all Central Asia. In accordance with his plans, the mosque and medresseh, which are certainly among the best buildings of their period in Central Asia, were duly completed and work begun on the minaret. But, before the minaret could be finished, fate intervened. Madamin Khan, who had been unfortunate enough to incur the hostility of the Russian Tsar, had, possibly by chance, but possibly not, an unhappy encounter with some Turkomans, who having cut his head off, sent it as an offering to the Shah of Persia — likewise no friend. And so the great minaret, magnificent as far as it went, remained unfinished, a massive but truncated stump, splendidly decorated with blue tiles and bearing to this day the name of Kalta Minar, the Short Minaret.

Of all the buildings in Khiva the oldest, or so it is said, is the domed Gumbaz or Mausoleum of Sheikh Seid Alauddin, which stands near the Ark by the West Gate of the city. This dates back to the fourteenth century, and for a long time lay half-buried in ancient debris, though eventually dug out and restored by one or other of the various architectural enthusiasts who reigned over Khiva during the nineteenth century.

But to my mind the finest and also one of the most interesting buildings in Khiva is the Mausoleum of Pahlavan Mahmud. With its beautiful octagonal blue-and-white dome, it stands in the southern quarter of the Inner City and was built between 1810 and 1835, mainly during the reign of Allah Kuli Khan. The painted majolica tiles which decorate the interior of the octagonal cupola are particularly splendid. From a relatively modest mausoleum, it gradually grew into a whole complex of buildings and subsequently served as the burial place of the reigning dynasty. Pahlavan Mahmud, whose name it bears and who lies buried in it under a handsome green-tiled tomb, lived in the fourteenth century. In addition to being a man of great holiness, he was also well known as a wrestler, a poet and a furrier, an interesting and I should imagine unusual combination of pursuits.

High above the Mausoleum of Pahlavan Mahmud towers the tapering, 150-foot minaret of Islam Khoja, built, together with the nearby mosque, by a Grand Vizir of that name in the reign of Asfendiar Khan (1910–20). Though doubtless not built with that intention, it is a fitting monument to mark the end of an era.

Immediately to the south of the Pahlavan Mahmud complex stands the Medresseh of Shirgazi Khan. This was built by the ruler of that name at the beginning of the eighteenth century, in order to celebrate a successful raid against Khorasan and also, to judge by some of the surviving inscriptions, for his own greater glorification ('Sun of the World', they run, 'Lion of God' ...). The Medresseh was the work, so the story goes, of the Persian prisoners brought back by Shirgazi Khan from Khorasan, on the understanding that as soon as they had finished their work they would be given their freedom. But, though the prisoners worked well, when the time came, the Khan equivocated and dragged things out, with the result that the prisoners rebelled and murdered him. Today the mosque is no more than a ruin and Shirgazi Khan lies buried in a modest grave nearby.

Adjoining Pahlavan Mahmud to the north is the Cathedral Mosque or Djuma. This does not compare in size or magnificence with the great cathedral mosques of Bokhara and Samarkand, and is mainly notable for the two hundred and twenty-seven carved wooden columns which support its wooden ceiling. These, as far as can be seen by the feeble light which filters into the interior through a series of hatches in the roof, are of varying designs and dates, some of them very old, though most of the actual structure seems to date from the end of the eighteenth century, when the mosque was largely rebuilt and the minaret added.

On the far side of the Inner City, perhaps three or four hundred yards from the Ark, a group of different buildings cluster round Palvan Darvaza, the impressive East Gate of the city, with its turreted gate-house. To fit them into the available space their builders relied on ingenuity rather than inspiration, and the proportions of some of the later buildings are inclined to be cramped and bear witness to makeshift expedients. Here, just outside the rectangle of the walls, are the caravanserai and covered bazaar built at the beginning of the nineteenth century in the reign of Allah Kuli Khan. This was where the merchants, having finally reached Khiva, rested and displayed their goods for sale. Nearby is the beautifully decorated mosque which bears the name of Allah Kuli Khan, as well as another, older shrine the Ak-Mechet or Blue Mosque, and also the Mosque of Kutlug Murad. Here too, complete with vestibule, soaping room, hot room and cold plunge, are the baths built two centuries earlier in 1657 by Abulgazi Khan to celebrate his son Anusha Mohammed's timely victory over the Bokharans, who had made a surprise attack on Khiva. Here, finally, is the new palace which Allah Kuli Khan built for himself between the years 1830 and 1838, the Tash Hauli or Stone House.

Hauli is the word used for the ordinary Khivan dwelling-house or manor, with its high outer wall designed to keep off marauders and inside its inner courtyard and northward-facing veranda or aivan, intended to catch the cool breezes. And this same pattern, on a larger scale, is reproduced in the Tash Hauli, the added *tash* (stone) being apparently justified by the fact that it is built of kiln-baked bricks in place of the sun-dried bricks or adobe used in most of the lesser buildings.

The Tash Hauli, which is contained within a solid outside wall, sufficient to keep both enemies and rebellious subjects at bay, consists of three main enclosed courtyards loosely linked with each other by winding passages (there seems to have been little or no overall architectural planning) and used, respectively, the first for a harem, the second for banquets, audiences and other state occasions, and the third as a court of justice. Giving on to the courtyards are a number of two-storied buildings, the rooms on the upper floor opening on to a gallery, supported by finely carved wooden columns. This pattern is varied by aivans which reach the whole height of the buildings and are also supported by tall carved wooden columns.

Wood-carving has always been a native Khivan art, and many of the columns are magnificent. All the buildings are lavishly decorated with majolica tiles, for the most part blue or white, bearing stylized floral or geometric designs.

As in the smaller houses, all the aivans face north, being carefully designed to catch any cool breezes in the hot weather and channel them into the rooms within. In winter, on the other hand, low brick platforms in the courtyards provided a base for the yurts or felt tents, heated by braziers, in which the Khan and his entourage, reverting to the habits of their nomad forebears, sought refuge from the cold. Reaching Khiva in mid-January, I could readily appreciate the need for them.

Standing on the ruins of the Ark and looking out over the brightly coloured minarets and domes of the walled city, and beyond them to the black sands of the dreaded Kara Kum, or wandering through the empty courtyards of the Tash Hauli and admiring the relics of General Kaufmann's conquest now displayed there, it is still possible to gain some idea of what Khiva must have been like in 1873, when the Russian troops first burst into the city after their spectacular approach march across three hundred miles of howling desert.

Mr Januarius Aloysius MacGahan, the enterprising special correspondent of the *New York Herald*, who, after a fantastic journey across the Kara Kum, had managed to get there at the psychological moment, thereby bringing off a phenomenal scoop, has left a vivid description of the scene. General Kaufmann, he tells us, after his famous march, entered Khiva in triumph with drums beating and colours flying, while a band played the Imperial Anthem. Meanwhile, from the other side of the city, came the sound of firing. Disregarding the city's surrender, young Colonel Skobelyov and a number of kindred spirits, under General Veryovkin's command, had chosen this moment to take Khiva by storm from the north and were even now fighting their way into the centre of the city, hotly opposed by some equally bellicose Turkomans. Just in time the order was given to withdraw, and General Kaufmann, followed by the Grand Duke Nicholas and Prince Eugene of Leuchtenberg, was enabled to continue his dignified progress between bowing rows of bearded Khivans towards the Tash Hauli, which Colonel Skobelyov, sword in hand, had only a few moments earlier taken by storm under a hail of bullets.

On reaching the Palace gate with its twin turrets, Kaufmann dismounted and made his way on foot through a series of passages and rooms to the

The Pilgrim
Urgut

The Grand Mufti and his Imams

◄ On the move

A veiled woman

Tashkent: the wedding feast

and the four grandfathers

Khiva: view from the Ark, ▶
Kalta Minar and
medresseh of Madamin Khan

Khiva   Icham Kala

The Khan's Palace

Khiva: the Khan's Palace

Khiva   Dishan Kala

Palace Gate
A gate of the Old City

A Khivan

Tajikstan: the foothills of the Pamirs   Dushambe: the Mosque ▶

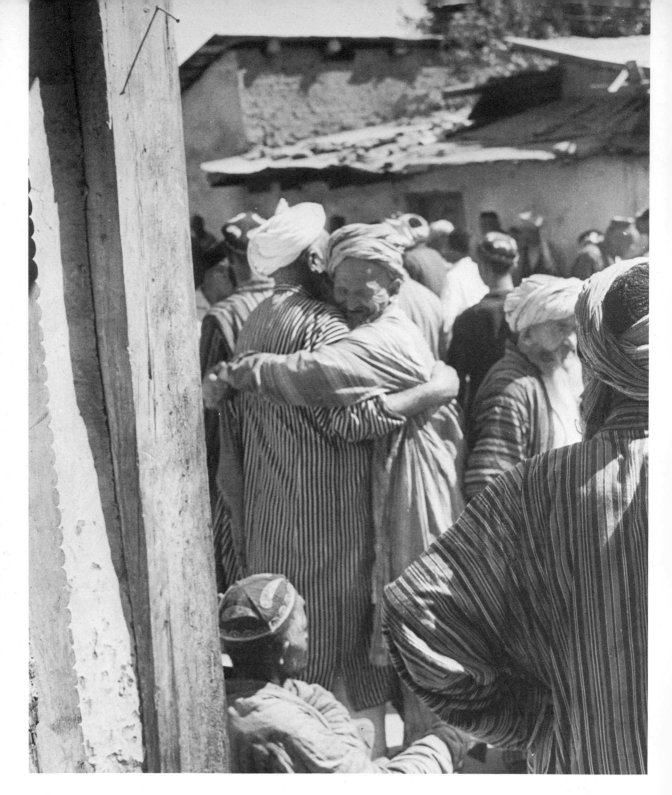

Dushambe: outside the Mosque

Tajikstan: the Pamirs

A Tajik

A Tajik girl

Penjikent

A Turkmen

Turkmenistan: the Mausoleum of Khan Abul Kazim-Babul

Grand Court of the Palace. On its southern side was the Grand Hall of State, an open veranda thirty feet high, flanked on both hands by towers ornamented with blue and green tiles, its roof supported by slender pillars of carved wood. Here, where the Khan had been accustomed to dispense justice, Kaufmann and his suite now flung themselves down to rest, while the band struck up an air from Offenbach's *Belle Hélène* and one of the Khan's ministers brought them iced water, wheaten cakes, cherries and apricots. 'With which', writes MacGahan, 'we merrily proceeded to refresh ourselves.' Later the enterprising MacGahan was to pay a midnight visit, revolver in hand, to the Khan's harem, with the firm intention of rescuing an eighteen-year-old beauty, whom he had caught sight of, gazing, as he thought, mournfully, through the gate, but who, on his arrival, burst into girlish giggles and promptly made him a pot of tea.

Right up to the time of its capture by the Russians, Khiva had been the centre of a flourishing slave-trade. Indeed the five thousand Russian slaves who still languished there were one of the chief causes of the Imperial Government's quarrel with the Khan. A male Russian, sound in wind and limb, could be counted on to fetch about 80 tillas, or considerably less than one pound sterling in the open market. Persian women, on the other hand, were considered superior to Russians and consequently fetched a rather higher price. The slaves, who constituted such a vital part of the Khivan economy, were brought in for the most part by Turkomen tribesmen, who earned their living by raiding caravans on their way across the desert. Their victims did not, however, always reach Khiva alive or, if they did, did not remain alive for long after their arrival. The Hungarian traveller Vambery, who reached Khiva disguised as a dervish in 1863, has a gruesome tale to tell of the arrival of one such raiding party. Of three hundred prisoners, some were chained by the neck and led away in batches to be sold as slaves, while others, as he watched, were hanged or beheaded. Some of the older prisoners just had their eyes gouged out, and Vambery describes how, after they had been blinded, the old men were set free and, groping around with their hands, tried to get to their feet, but in their agony fell over each other, their heads bumping together as they did so. Next day another newly returned raiding party came to claim the rewards of their prowess. These were gold-embroidered robes and were known variously as 'twelve-head', 'twenty-head' or even 'forty-head' robes according to their quality. The raiders who claimed them first emptied from the sacks they had brought with them on to the floor of the Treasury the requisite number of severed human heads. These an accountant kicked into a pile, and in return the raiders were given official receipts, which they duly handed in in exchange for a robe of appropriate quality.

In 1876, three years after its capture by the Russians, Khiva was visited by another indefatigable traveller from the west, Captain Fred Burnaby of the Blues, a gigantic cavalry officer who had suddenly conceived the idea of a trip to Khiva while glancing through a newspaper the year before at Khartoum, on his way back from the White Nile, where he had gone to interview 'Chinese Gordon', the newly appointed Governor of the Equatorial Provinces.

In addition to being a soldier and a traveller, Burnaby also won fame as a war correspondent in the Balkans, as a cross-Channel balloonist, and as a Tory Parliamentary candidate, running in double harness with Lord Randolph Churchill. In *A Ride to Khiva*, which, despite an unkind review from Henry James, who called its author 'opaque in intellect but indomitable in muscle', quickly became a runaway best-seller and also put Khiva firmly on the map as far as the British public were concerned, he describes his journey across the steppes in the jaunty style of the period. His narrative carries the reader agreeably along from the moment when, having declined the offer of a friend in the Foot Guards to accompany him and finally decided to leave behind his soldier servant ('faithful fellow'), he started off alone from 'the Victoria Station' by the night mail *en route* for St Petersburg, complete with trooper's hold-all (knife, fork and spoon), waterproof sleeping-bag, money-belt, supply of Cockle's Pills, air mattress, flannel shirts, fur-lined boots and 'four pairs of the thickest Scotch fishing stockings', until the moment two months later when he rode into Khiva, followed by his newly acquired Tartar servant, his guide and three camels, to be received with some ceremony by the Khan, still painfully adjusting himself to the loss of his independence and clearly still rather resentful at the British Government's failure to come to his rescue.

Burnaby's book is extremely readable, being full of improvised dinner parties and 'blue eyed sirens', of mazurkas and caviar and vodka, of wolves and comic Tartar waiters and drunken cossacks, of knife-fights and floggings and 'well-turned out troikas', of horse- and camel-coping, of days hunting in improbable places, and duels, and 'effeminate boys dressed a little like women', of witty exchanges with Russian officers and other travellers encountered *en route*, and of endless other entertaining episodes and interludes. One can easily see that it might not have had much of a message for Henry James. It leaves one, however, with an engaging portrait of its picturesque and resilient author, who was to meet a heroic end nine years later in the ill-fated skirmish at Abu Klea, serving with the rank of colonel in the expeditionary force which had been sent, too late, to relieve General Gordon at Khartoum. 'The Gatling's jammed', wrote Sir Henry Newbolt shortly afterwards in commemoration of this sad event, 'and the Colonel dead, And the regiment blind with dust and smoke.'

Like Bokhara, the Khanate of Khiva enjoyed a brief return of independence after the Bolshevik Revolution. But in 1922 the Khan, like his Bokharan neighbour, was driven into exile and his Khanate transformed into the Soviet Republic of Khorezm, which in due course was absorbed into the larger Soviet Republic of Uzbekistan. Today Khiva is a ghost-town, and the real life of the district carries on in the neighbouring town of New Urgench, and on the thriving cotton plantations and sheep farms of the oasis, which, with improved systems of irrigation, is rapidly growing in size and fertility.

12 *Tajiks and Turkmens*

Racially almost all the peoples of Soviet Central Asia have a strong Turanian strain and the languages they speak are akin to Turkish. The Tajiks, on the other hand, who live high up in the valleys and foothills of the Pamirs, where the frontiers of the Soviet Union converge with those of China, Afghanistan, Pakistan and India, are an exception. By race, language, and civilization, they are close, not to the Turks, but to the Persians, and, when I visited Central Asia before the war, it was said that the Tajiks still managed to smuggle small sums of money across the frontier as their tribute to the Aga Khan, the head of the Ismaili sect and, as we have seen, the lineal descendant of the Old Man of the Mountain. The idea of this little Persian enclave, right up in the High Pamir, has always intrigued me, and I had long aspired to visit Tajikstan. But it was only recently that I was able to satisfy my curiosity by dropping off there on my way from Tashkent to Turkmenistan.

Dushambe, the capital of the Soviet Socialist Republic of Tajikstan, is only a short flight from Tashkent. I arrived there after dark. Feeling hungry after my journey, I went down to the dining-room of the aggressively modern hotel to get something to eat and immediately found myself once again involved in a wedding, a Russian one this time, the bride and bridegroom both being young technologists who had come to Tajikstan from Leningrad. Under the star-spangled ceiling of the new ballroom the vodka was flowing freely and the twist was being danced with a zest that would not have disgraced the Peppermint Lounge. Most of the men wore tight trousers and tremendous sideburns, while the ladies' gold lamé skirts were worn far above the knees. Against the blare of jazz and through a haze of vodka I did my best to justify American policy in Vietnam in a series of disjointed but lively exchanges.

There were quite a number of Tajiks in the party, and the next day I met a lot more. They are a charming and highly civilized people, with a well-developed sense of humour, and I took to them at once. Dushambe, which was only a village before the Revolution, is now a completely modern town of a quarter of a million inhabitants, including many Uzbeks and Russians, and is the centre of a thriving cotton industry. It has a Park of Rest and Culture with a lake for bathing and boating and a splendid speedway leading right up into the mountains. It also has, so the local mullah told me, over the usual cup of green tea, four mosques, as against one before the Revolution. Certainly the one I visited was thronged by a numerous and devout congregation. And afterwards there was a large and vociferous gathering of bearded and turbaned elders in the street outside who offered a striking contrast to the gathering of the night before in the hotel ballroom.

Ninety-three per cent of Tajikstan is mountainous. Indeed it can boast one or two of the highest mountains in the world — peaks that rival Everest and Annapurna. Hydro-electric power, not surprisingly, plays an important part in Tajikstan's industrial development, the rate of which, one is proudly, if rather naively told, exceeds that of the United States.

From the ruins of the ancient town of Penjikent, also in Tajikstan, on the Uzbek border a few hours' drive south-east from Samarkand, you look across to the foothills of the Pamirs, far away to the south where China meets Afghanistan. Penjikent, a Sogdian settlement, believed to date back to the fifth or sixth century of our era, was deserted by its inhabitants after the Arab invasion of Central Asia in the eighth century. From recent discoveries it seems as though, in the last resort, the natives had taken to the hills under their Prince, Divashtich, and there made a final stand against the Arab invaders in defence of a fortified position on the neighbouring Mug Kalà or Mount Mug. Here it was that an important cache of documents, no doubt made at that time, was discovered only a few years back.

Penjikent itself has now been thoroughly excavated. Its site covers an area of nearly fifty acres, and to the trained eye of the archaeologist reveals an intricate network of intersecting streets, a market-place, various places of worship, and large numbers of dwelling-houses both great and small. As the city, once abandoned, was never re-occupied or re-built, many of the walls are still standing and even the uninitiated can, with an effort of the imagination, trace the main outlines of the settlement. The latest excavations have produced large quantities of bronze ornaments, pottery, carving, domestic utensils and other artifacts, as well as a number of not unimpressive wall-paintings, depicting battle- and hunting-scenes and a variety of fairy tales and legends connected with various religious cults, from all of which the experts have been able to piece together a remarkably complete picture of life in pre-Moslem Central Asia.

From Dushambe I continued my journey westwards, along the blue line of hills which mark the Persian frontier, to Ashkhabad in Turkmenistan. To the north, as we flew, the black sands of the great Kara Kum desert stretched away endlessly in the heat haze to the Oxus and the Sea of Aral.

The Turkmens, as we have seen, were the last of the races of Central Asia to fall under Russian domination, their main force being massacred by General Skobelyov after the storming of their fortress of Geok Tepe in 1881, and the remainder capitulating a couple of years later. What was left of Geok Tepe can still be seen some thirty miles north-west of Ashkhabad. The older parts of Ashkhabad, with their avenues of neat bungalows, still have, like the original Russian quarter of Tashkent, the air of a garrison town. To this day the Turkmens, grandsons of the tribesmen who fought with such ferocity against the Russians, have a wild look, as they squat in the bazaars and at the street corners in their enormous sheepskin busbies. By tradition they are nomads, pasturing their flocks in whatever parts of their vast but arid country offer the best prospect of survival, and it is here that some of the finest Karakul and Persian lamb-skins are produced. So also, strangely enough, are what we call Bokhara carpets, which in reality have always been woven by the Turkmens in their desert encampments and only brought into the bazaars of Bokhara to be sold. Now they are made, still on handlooms, in Ashkhabad, the price charged being about the same as in London or New York.

A few miles outside the town I found, and, after some argument inspected, an ancient monument, the fifteenth-century mosque or mausoleum of Khan Abdul Kasim Babur, a local potentate. It and the fortress inside which it was built turned out, when we got there, to have been pretty well finished off by an eighteenth-century earthquake, although it is still possible to identify two white dragons on a blue ground above the sixty-foot arch. However, despite seismic and ideological vicissitudes, it seems still to have retained its sanctity, and people who mind about these things are to this day taken out there to be buried.

On the way back to Ashkhabad we drove past the race-course. 'Races this afternoon', said my Turkmen friends. 'You shouldn't miss them.' But the Aeroflot timetable intervened, and by the time the Turkmen jockeys with their fur busbies and vicious-looking whips were under starter's orders, I was airborne and soaring 30,000 feet above the green metallic waters of the Caspian.

13 *Outer Mongolia*

Right at the other end of Central Asia from the Caspian, far to the east of Kazakstan, lies Mongolia. For centuries it was a kind of no-man's-land between Russia and China. But although Inner Mongolia has now become part of China, Outer Mongolia, or, to give it its proper name, the Mongolian People's Republic, is not, and never has been, part of the Soviet Union. Communism came to the Mongols, it is true, in much the same way as it came to most of the outlying Soviet Republics — after a period of turmoil and civil war, followed by the decisive intervention of the Red Army. But, though a close alliance between the two countries was at once concluded, Mongolia remained officially independent of Russia and did not become, as she well might have done, one of the member republics of the Soviet Union, with which she shared a common frontier some 2,400 miles in length. Rather she remained a partial buffer, sometimes convenient and sometimes less so, between Russia and her neighbour China, with whom she shared an even longer frontier, stretching across mountains and deserts for no less than 3,800 miles. And this state of affairs, through various vicissitudes, has somehow endured ever since.

My reason for including some account of Mongolia in this volume, which is primarily concerned with Soviet Central Asia, lies more in its past history than in the close links which today bind it to the Soviet Union. In seeking to trace the story of Central Asia and the Caucasus, or for that matter of Russia itself, it is impossible to leave out the Mongols. And, having followed the fortunes of Jenghiz Khan and those who came after him as far as I have, it seemed unreasonable to omit all further reference to the subsequent development and history of their country.

As far as I can remember, I first became aware of the existence of Outer Mongolia as a country more than thirty-five years ago, in Moscow. Idly looking through the list of my fellow members of the diplomatic corps not long after my arrival there, I came upon the Legation of the People's Republic of Outer Mongolia, headed by the Minister, Monsieur Sambuu, and at the next official reception I was able to identify him by his characteristically Mongolian countenance and his charmingly Mongolian-looking wife.

But that was all. In those days Great Britain did not recognize Outer Mongolia. In fact no one did except the Soviet Union. And so, in diplomatic circles, Monsieur and Madame Sambuu led socially isolated lives, as the representatives in the Soviet Union of what was then the only other Communist country in the world (or almost the only one, for there was then also the neighbouring Republic of Tannu Tuva, which since seems somehow to have disappeared).

Nor, supposing that one wanted to, was it at all clear in those days how one could get to Outer Mongolia. The Trans-Siberian Railway, which I had successfully used as a jumping-off point for various other expeditions, seemed to miss it. As for Dr Sambuu, he showed no inclination to issue visas, nor indeed to have any dealings whatever with his diplomatic colleagues.

A rather half-hearted attempt to drift in one autumn by way of Siberia and the Altai Mountains ended a hundred miles or so short of my objective in a sea of mud and a dishearteningly continuous downpour of rain. And so for a quarter of a century Outer Mongolia remained for me a name on the map, and on the numerous large and brightly coloured postage stamps issued by an enterprising Outer Mongolian Minister of Posts and Telegraphs.

But then suddenly, thirty years later, in the nineteen-sixties, Mongolia was in the news. (It was Outer Mongolia no longer. Inner Mongolia had in the meantime been eaten by China. So now there was one.) Mongolia, we learned, had, at her fifth attempt, joined the United Nations. Dr Sambuu, my former colleague, having written a book entitled *Advice to Herdsmen*, had become President of the Republic and was now busy writing a *History of Religion*. The Americans were thinking of recognizing Mongolia. Great Britain had actually done so, though ambassadors had not yet been exchanged. The famous traveller Peter Fleming had applied for a Mongolian visa and been refused, owing to his notorious family connection with that enemy of the people James Bond. In Mongolia there were dinosaurs' eggs 90 million years old. Mongolia was on everyone's lips. In Mongolia the sun shone 300 days out of 365. Where, my wife and I asked ourselves, can we go for Whitsun? There could only be one answer.

The elegant little black dress worn by the sensationally attractive Mongolian lady across the breakfast table at Irkutsk Airport could only have come from Fifth Avenue. Having flown the 3,000 miles from Moscow between midnight and six in the morning, without the sun either going down or rising, I was feeling slightly disembodied and was comforted to be addressed by so charming a person in faultless American, and to learn that she was a member of the Mongolian Delegation to the United Nations. With her and her children we clambered hopefully on board the waiting Mongolair aircraft and we soon looking down on Lake Baikal.

About Lake Baikal I seemed, I reflected, to have accumulated a certain amount of rather disparate information. Not only is it the deepest lake in the world, but it is yearly getting deeper. It is 400 miles long, the length of England, in fact longer. It contains one-fifth of all the fresh water in the world. It freezes regularly every year on the same day, the 26th of January. And, last but not least, it contains no less than 240 different varieties of shrimp, many of them delicious and for the most part unique to its waters.

But soon Lake Baikal, shrimps and all, was out of sight. Next came some wooded mountains, then prolonged turbulence, when Mongolian air-hostesses in national dress handed round boiled sweets and paper bags, and one tried to keep one's attention on one's book. Then a lot more mountains – the Khangai of Northern Mongolia – and we were coming in to land at Ulan Bator, the capital of the Mongolian People's Republic.

Ulan Bator, or Red Hero, is by any standards a very long way away: 1,000 miles from Peking; 1,800 miles from the Arctic Ocean; 2,000 miles from Delhi; 3,000 miles from Moscow; even today these are considerable distances. It is also the capital of an extremely large country. From east to west, Mongolia measures almost 1,500 miles, and from north to south just on 800. In area it is about the size of France, Germany, Italy and Great Britain put together.

One is conscious of its size and remoteness as soon as one gets there. A few miles out from Ulan Bator you lose sight of the ranges of mountains to the north, and the steppe begins: a vast expanse of green rolling country stretching away to a distant horizon of hills. One is conscious, too, of its emptiness.

We only caught a passing glimpse of Ulan Bator from the windows of the shiny black Soviet car which met us at the airport. We had been taken in hand on arrival by the head of the Mongol Tourist Organization, Madame Solj, a plump, vivacious lady, who made a little Russian go a long way, and by Mr Orchibal, a young man from the Ministry of Foreign Affairs, who combined a good knowledge of English with infinite patience and a keen sense of humour, which were to make him an ideal travelling companion.

I had asked the Mongolian Ambassador in Moscow, when he gave us our visas, to reserve accommodation for us at a hotel. What would it be like? It turned out to be a large, rather nice, modern building, with balconies overlooking a secluded valley in the hills above the town. It had been built and equipped by imported Chinese labour, and the luxurious suite of bedroom, bathroom and drawing-room into which we were shown was furnished with attractive Chinese silks and carpets and well-made, well-designed modern furniture.

No sooner had we settled in than we were summoned to the first of a long series of copious Soviet-style meals, interspersed with strange but not unsavoury Mongolian specialities, including innumerable different kinds of highly spiced meat balls and dumplings, known as *pilmeni*, and washed down (as they needed to be) with plenty of Mongolian vodka, Crimean port and Armenian brandy. There was no one else staying in the hotel. The long corridors echoed emptily. The bill, as I was later to discover to my dismay, came to the equivalent of 100 American dollars a day. But our first twenty-four hours were unmarred by any such unpleasant shock.

From our mountain valley we sallied forth daily in our black limousine in search of enlightenment and instruction. Apart from a lama temple or two, Ulan Bator is a completely modern town with a rapidly growing population of more than 300,000, where substantial blocks of modern flats are fast replacing the rather untidy groups of tents which still cluster on the outskirts. In addition to the usual imposing government buildings common to all Communist countries and a massive mausoleum containing the bodies of Sukhe Bator and Choibalsan, the two heroes of the Revolution of 1921, Ulan Bator also boasts a well-stocked department store, an opera house, a university, an academy of science, a grand hotel, a stadium, a large new hospital, and a number of up-to-date factories, mostly geared to Mongolia's pastoral economy and including a meat-canning factory, a tannery, a boot-and-shoe factory, and a wool mill, equipped with the latest British textile machinery.

While we were in Ulan Bator, we visited textile mills, housing estates, hospitals, infant schools, lama temples, institutes of veterinary science, centres of acupuncture, libraries, museums, and the Great State Department Store. We were taken to the wrestling and the elections and the cinema and the State Circus, where we saw jugglers and acrobats and exotic dancers in

G-strings and a performing white yak in golden harness. We called on the Prime Minister and the Chief Lama and the Commander-in-Chief of the Army and the Rector of the University and the President of the Academy of Science, and an extremely well-built young lady who danced at the circus, and an ordinary family living in an ordinary apartment.

But we did not want to spend all our time in the city. After some pretty determined haggling I managed to hire, for a mere 500 dollars, a Soviet-made Jeep and a driver, and we set out to view the remains of Jenghiz Khan's ancient capital of Karakorum, a couple of hundred miles away across the steppe. On his knees the driver carried an antiquated sporting gun, fully loaded, in readiness, he told us, to despatch such wolves as we might encounter. (He only got one shot and missed.)

In such an immense country a population of not much more than a million is thinly spread. A vast expanse of green rolling steppe stretches away to a distant horizon of hills. In a hundred miles you may meet another car. Or you may not. Probably you will meet just a shepherd with his sheep, or a herd or two of horses or cattle; or a little group of exotic-looking, high-cheekboned nomads on the march, with all their worldly belongings loaded on to a string of dromedaries. But on all sides the steppe is alive with small furry animals, marmots, mice, jerboas, popping inquisitively in and out of their holes and scuttling rapidly back again—a tempting target for the eagles and other great birds of prey that hover menacingly overhead.

Here and there as we drove we came on a little cluster of *gers*, the traditional Mongolian round white tents of felt stretched over a collapsible wooden framework, in which the bulk of the population still live and which they carry with them on their camels when they move. It was in these that we paused on our way to get out of the cold and into a warm Mongol family atmosphere, and eat strange meals of tea and cheese and great bowls of *airag*, or fermented mare's milk, in the centre of a circle of friendly, grinning, curious faces. (As a drink, incidentally, fermented mare's milk is strongly to be recommended. It is effervescent, more than slightly intoxicating, and a sovereign remedy, by all accounts, for rheumatism and tuberculosis.)

In short, nothing much has changed since Friar William of Rubruck visited Mongolia in 1255. 'Nowhere', writes Friar William, 'have they fixed dwelling-places, nor do they know where their next will be ... every captain knows the limits of his pasture lands and where to graze in winter and summer, spring and autumn. For in winter they go down to warmer regions in the south: in summer they go up to cooler pastures towards the north. The pasture lands without water they graze over in winter when there is snow there, for the snow serveth them as water. They set up the dwelling in which they sleep on a circular frame of interlaced sticks converging into a little round hoop on the top from which projects above a collar as a chimney, and this they cover over with white felt. The felt around this collar on top they decorate with various pretty designs in colour ... And they make these houses so large that they are sometimes thirty feet in width.'

Airag or *kumiss* was already a popular drink in the thirteenth century. 'In summer', writes Friar William, 'they care only for *cosmos*. There is always *cosmos* near the house, before the entry door and beside it stands a guitar-player with his guitar ... And when the master begins to drink then one of the attendants cries with a loud voice, "Ha!" and the guitarist strikes his guitar ... and when the master has drunken, then the attendant cries as before and the guitarist stops. This *cosmos*, which is mare's milk, is made in this wise. They stretch a long rope on the ground fixed to two stakes stuck in the ground, and to this rope they tie toward the third hour the colts of the mares they want to milk. Then the mothers stand near their foal, and allow themselves to be quietly milked; and if one be too wild, then a man takes the colt and brings it to her, allowing it to suck a little; then he takes it away and the milker takes its place. When they have got together a great quantity of milk, which is as sweet as cow's as long as it is fresh, they pour it into a big skin or bottle, and they set to churning it with a stick prepared for that purpose, and which is as big as a man's head at its lower extremity and hollowed out; and when they have beaten it sharply it begins to boil up like a new wine and to sour or ferment, and they continue to churn it until they have extracted the butter. Then they taste it, and when it is mildly pungent, they drink it. It is pungent on the tongue like rape wine when drunk, and when a man has finished drinking, it leaves a taste of milk of almonds on the tongue, and it makes the inner man most joyful and also intoxicates weak heads, and greatly provokes urine. They also make *caracosmos*, that is "black *cosmos*", for the use of the great lords.'

Marco Polo, writing twenty or thirty years later, gives a similar account. 'They spend two or three months', he writes, 'climbing steadily and grazing as they go, because if they confined their grazing to one spot there would not be grass enough for the multitude of their flocks. They have circular houses made of wood and covered with felt, which they carry about with

116

them on four-wheeled wagons wherever they go. For the framework of rods is so neatly and skilfully constructed that it is light to carry. And every time they unfold their house and set it up, the door is always facing south. They also have excellent two-wheeled carts covered with black felt, of such good design that if it rained all the time the rain would never wet anything in the cart. These are drawn by oxen and camels and serve to convey their wives and children, their utensils and such provisions as they require. You should know', he continues, 'that they drink mare's milk, but they subject it to a process that makes it like white wine and very good to drink, and they call it *koumiss*.'

Strictly speaking there are no proper roads in Mongolia – just a whole series of widely divergent tracks across the plain from which you hopefully select the most promising. Further south, the steppe turns gradually into desert or *gobi*, a mixture, like most deserts, of patches of scrub, salt flats and sand dunes, and great stretches of nothing in particular, turned into a wilderness seven hundred years ago, they say, by the trampling of Jenghiz Khan's myriad cavalry.

After stopping repeatedly on the way to film the great herds of horses that drift about the steppe and then getting hopelessly lost in the darkness among the innumerable divergent tracks, we did not complete the first stage of our journey until five the following morning, only to find, to our amazement, that after crossing two hundred miles of steppe, we were staying in yet another luxury suite with sitting-room and bathroom attached, and a Chinese toothbrush and tube of toothpaste laid out for each of us in case we had left ours at home. After a few hours' sleep we set out again for Karakorum, the Black Camp of Jenghiz Khan.

On the way we stopped off at a farm where we saw more horses than ever, took a ride round ourselves, and witnessed a fantastic display of rough-riding. The Mongols have remained a nation of horsemen. It was they, they claim, who invented the saddle, who practically invented riding; in fact, it was in Mongolia that the first horse made its appearance. To this day, each Mongolian man, woman and child is ready to jump on to a horse and gallop off, and they expect their visitors to do the same. Nor is there any lack of mounts in a country where there are far more horses than people. The Mongols love horses. Racing, after wrestling, is their most popular pastime, the horses entered being ridden over a twenty-mile course by children of both sexes aged between six and ten. Mare's milk is their favourite drink. Their national emblem is a horseman galloping into the rising sun, and on the main square of the capital the equestrian statue of Sukhe Bator, the Revolutionary Hero of 1921, prances magnificently.

The equestrian proficiency of the Mongols has not been without its influence on Mongolian history. With his hordes of Huns on their sturdy little ponies, Attila, the Scourge of God, emerging from innermost Asia in the fifth century A.D., threatened the frontiers of the Roman Empire, while at the same time other Hun tribes, turning eastwards, invaded China. It was largely his skill as a cavalry commander and the mobility and endurance of his cavalry that made Jenghiz the most formidable military phenomenon of his age eight centuries later, and enabled him and his immediate successors to become in a very short time masters of three-quarters of the known world.

Marco Polo, who saw the Mongols in action, gives an eye-witness account of their strategy and tactics. 'When they join battle with their enemies', he writes, 'these are the tactics by which they prevail. They are never ashamed to have recourse to flight. They manœuvre freely, shooting at the enemy, now from this quarter, now from that. They have trained their horses so well that they wheel this way or that as quickly as a dog would do. When they are pursued and take to flight, they fight as well and as effectively as when they are face to face with the enemy. When they are fleeing at top speed, they twist round with their bows and let fly their arrows to such good purpose that they kill the horses of the enemy and the riders too. When the enemy thinks he has routed and crushed them, then he is lost; for he finds his horses killed and not a few of his men. As soon as the Tartars decide that they have killed enough of the pursuing horses and horsemen, they wheel round and attack and acquit themselves so well and so courageously that they gain a complete victory. By these tactics they have already won many battles and conquered many nations.'

But the Mongol Empire did not last for long. Not much more than a century after Jenghiz's conquest of China, the Chinese, as we have seen, drove back the Mongols, and, turning the tables on them, utterly destroyed their capital of Karakorum. Today, as we found when we finally arrived there, nothing of all its former magnificence remains but a solitary stone tortoise, derelict and disconsolate, on to which every now and then a passer-by drops a pebble or two out of a vague deference to its presumed holiness. Having added ours to the pile, we went on our way. Of the once great city with its temples and palaces and pleasure-domes not one stone stands upon another. They were taken, it is said, in the sixteenth century to build the neighbouring Lamaist monastery of Erdeni Dzu, now in its turn falling into decay, with a solitary lama and, we supposed, his little daughter in attendance in its grass-grown courts.

For six centuries after the fall of Karakorum, nothing much was heard of the Mongols. First Inner and then Outer Mongolia became a part of China. Lamaist Buddhism, introduced from Tibet by Jenghiz's grandson Kublai Khan, grew to be the dominant influence, and under Chinese suzerainty the Bogda Gegen or Living Buddha of Urga became in effect the ruler of the country. The result was the complete transformation of a once warlike, dynamic people. At the beginning of the present century a quarter of the national wealth belonged to the monasteries, and 40 per cent of the adult male population were celibate, unproductive lamas. With their dead hand on education and medicine and their resistance on doctrinal grounds to agriculture, mining and industry, the lamas managed through the centuries to keep Mongolia in a state of medieval stagnation, while the population dwindled over the years to only a few hundred thousand.

During the latter half of the nineteenth century there had, however, been an important change in Mongolia's international situation. Ever since the annexation of the Amur region by the Tsars in 1858, Mongolia had shared a 1,500-mile frontier with Russia. From a loosely held bastion of China, the Russians, by a policy of gradual penetration and by means of judiciously distributed sums of gold roubles, had succeeded in making it, first, into a kind of no-man's-land between the two empires, and next into what, though nominally an autonomous region of China under the suzerainty of Peking, was in practice a Russian protectorate, where everyone, from the living Buddha downwards, literally worshipped at the shrine of the Russian Tsar, and where devout crowds of Mongols would run after the Russian Consul whenever he went out, in order to breath in the sacred clouds of dust that blew up from under the wheels of his motor-car.

Such Mongols as gave the matter any serious thought were inclined to welcome this development, in the belief that they had less to fear from Moscow, which was further away, than from Peking, which was near by and more inclined to impinge on their affairs, in particular by promoting Chinese immigration into Inner Mongolia. By the turn of the century the Russians had come to be regarded, strangely enough, almost as liberators.

One of the consequences of the Chinese Revolution of 1911 was to loosen still further Mongolia's links with Peking, and so to arouse in

Mongolia a new national consciousness and further sharpen the emphasis on autonomy. In 1915 the tripartite Treaty of Kyakhta formalized the new position by officially granting Outer Mongolia autonomy under Chinese suzerainty, but in effect merely confirming the Russian protectorate, and thus in a way preparing the ground for what was to follow. But the real turning-point in Mongolian affairs came two years later, with the Russian Revolution of 1917 and the events that followed it.

The immediate effect of the Bolshevik Revolution and ensuing civil war was to weaken Russian influence throughout the Far East. Towards the end of 1919 the Chinese government took advantage of this to denounce the Treaty of Kyakhta and reassert their absolute sovereignty over Outer Mongolia. Neither the Mongols themselves nor the new Soviet Russian government raised any effective objection, and the Chinese set up at Urga a highly repressive government under General Hsü Shu-Tseng, better known as Little Hsü.

It was not long, however, before the harshness of Little Hsü's regime provoked a reaction. Early in 1920 the breath of insurrection touched Mongolia, and a revolutionary movement sprang into being in Urga, led by a young Mongol cavalryman called Sukhe Bator or Sukhe the Hero. In touch with him was Hutuktu Khan, the blind Bogda Gegen or Living Buddha, who, for reasons of his own, was also anxious to get rid of Little Hsü and the Chinese. In the spring of 1920 a secret emissary of the Comintern visited the Holy City, and on 15 July Sukhe Bator rode out of Urga, bound for Irkutsk in Siberia and carrying, it is said, a special message for Lenin in the hollowed-out handle of his riding whip. He also carried with him a request for aid which bore the sacred seal of the Bogda Gegen.

14 *The Mad Baron*

While Sukhe Bator was in Irkutsk, however, negotiating with the Soviet authorities for help, events took a different turn. There was a change of government in Peking. In Urga the rule of Little Hsü came to an abrupt end and suddenly chaos ensued. It is at this stage that a new and strange character appears on the scene: a tall, red-haired, white-faced, Imperial Russian cavalry officer in his early thirties, of part-Baltic and part-Hungarian extraction, by religion a Buddhist, with long, thin fingers, a small head set on broad shoulders, a high-pitched, hysterical voice, piercing, watery-blue eyes, one set lower than the other, pale lips above a narrow chin, a straggling reddish moustache, a fearful sabre-cut across his forehead and manifestly paranoiac tendencies, usually believing himself to be a reincarnation of Jenghiz Khan or, in his less lucid moments, the God of War in person. Such was His Excellency Chiang Chün Major-General Baron Roman Fyodorovich von Ungern-Sternberg, the descendant of a long line of Baltic barons, crusaders, pirates and freebooters by sea and by land, carrying in their veins, their descendant proudly claimed, the blood of Attila's Huns, which gave him, or so he believed, a special affinity for Mongols and Mongolia. From under his overhanging brow his 'sharp, steely eyes' glared out at you 'like those of an animal from a cave'. The very sight of him, we are told, was enough to make a cold shiver run down one's spine.

Baron Ungern had started life as a cadet in the Imperial Russian Navy, but, feeling the need for more excitement, had made his way to the Far East and there joined the Transbaikal Cossacks. His military career had been marked by a series of illicit duels and other more scandalous episodes. 'A gentleman when sober', was the verdict of one of his brother officers, 'he was a wild beast when drunk.' Twice cashiered from the army, each time he somehow found his way back into it. Around the year 1912 he had spent some time on his own in Mongolia, fighting the Chinese and robbing caravans. The country and the people, he found, had the strongest possible appeal for him. In 1914 the outbreak of war had enabled him once more to force his way back into the army, and he had been sent to the German front. There the unfriendly attitude of his brother officers enraged him. He determined to show them what sort of a man he was. 'Dashing into battle like a lunatic', he was soon covered with decorations for gallantry and at thirty-three was a major-general. A sabre-cut on the head still further disturbed the balance of his mind. 'I venture to say', remarked a member of his entourage warningly to someone about to encounter him for the first time, 'that he is insane most of the time.'

In Siberia, whither Ungern had found his way after the Revolution, the civil war had ended earlier in 1920 with the victory of the Bolsheviks. But odd bands of marauding Tsarist White Guards, once part of the army commanded by the notorious half-Russian, half-Mongol Cossack Hetman Semyonov, were still at large in the area, living as best they could off the country. From these desperate men, with nothing whatever to lose and nothing much to hope for, and from any other likely recruits he could find among the human flotsam and jetsam adrift in the area, whether Mongols, Russians, Japanese, Chinese or Austro-Hungarian prisoners-of-war, Baron Ungern, who had latterly been serving under Semyonov, now raised a mixed irregular force under his own command. His aim was to found a vast Asiatic empire, as Jenghiz Khan had done, and then invade Europe at the head of his conquering hordes.

One of those thus recruited has left a first-hand account of Ungern's recruiting methods. The Baron was dressed, he tells us, in a dirty fur hat, a short Chinese jacket of cherry-red silk, blue uniform breeches and high Mongol boots. In his right hand he held the famous bamboo riding whip with which he would lash out savagely at those who aroused his fire. Going down the line of potential recruits, he would stop before each man in turn, look him in the face, hold his gaze for a few moments and then scream, in a high tenor: 'To the Army!' 'Back to the cattle!' Or simply: 'Liquidate!' All men with physical defects were immediately shot, the Baron, who believed implicitly in reincarnation, being convinced that he was doing them a kindness and helping them improve their chances next time round. He also, on principle, immediately killed all Jews, regardless of age, sex or ability. By the time each such inspection was completed hundreds of people had been slaughtered.

Baron Ungern's immediate aim was to make himself master of Outer Mongolia, where he firmly believed that he had a divine mission to fulfil. With the force he had recruited, he now crossed the Mongolian border and, after a long approach march, launched at the end of October 1920 a night attack on the Holy City of Urga. This was a failure. On reaching the outskirts of Urga, his troops found themselves caught in a withering cross-fire from the Chinese garrison, who were well dug in, relatively well armed, and outnumbered his forces ten to one. After suffering heavy losses, the Baron withdrew to the nearby hills. There he waited in a raging snowstorm for a favourable sign from the soothsayers who always accompanied him.

After five days of waiting, frozen almost to death, his men were desperate. But still there was no sign. On the sixth day the Baron led them once more against the entrenched Chinese. As one of his officers ruefully observes, the Baron's personal bravery was 'just a handicap to his subordinates'. For their part, these fought with the courage of despair and somehow managed to breach the enemy's defences. In the bloody battle that ensued the Chinese were beginning to get the worst of it and were on the point of evacuating the city. Then one Chinese officer, with the fatalism of his race, rallied his men for a last forlorn stand against the enemy. This, as it happened, turned the scales, and once again the Baron was obliged to give his troops the order to withdraw. He now fell back, first to Tirildja and then to the Kerulen River, where he settled down to await fresh reinforcements and regroup his forces before returning to the attack. In Urga, meanwhile, the Chinese tightened things up, resorting to still more drastic measures and imprisoning the Bogda Gegen and a number of other Mongol notables.

It was not until the end of January 1921 that Baron Ungern resumed the offensive. This time the soothsayers, in accordance with an ancient prophecy, had fixed the first day of February, the fifth day of the first moon, as the day on which his attack on the sacred city was to be launched. It was on this day, according to the old prophets, that the Living Buddha was to be liberated from his Chinese captors. On 22 January the Baron's force, which now numbered 1,700 men, set out from the Kerulen River on the long march across snowy, wolf-infested country to Urga.

Their stopping-places on the march were chosen in accordance with various ancient Mongolian prophecies, while the disposition of the units under the Baron's command was regulated by reference to the cracks in mutton-bones specially dried for this purpose in the ashes of their camp fires. In so doing the Baron was following an old Mongol custom. 'And as we were entering', wrote Friar William of Rubruck in 1253 of a visit to Möngke Khan, 'a servant came out, carrying some sheep's shoulder blades, burnt to a cinder, and I wondered greatly what he could do with them. When later on I enquired about it, I learnt that he does nothing in the world without first consulting the bones.' 'To the simple nomads', wrote one of Ungern's companions, 'it all seemed miraculous.' More convinced than ever that the Baron was, as they had been told, a reincarnation of Tzagan Burkhan, the God of war, specially sent down from heaven to lead them, they followed him blindly.

On 29 January the Baron's force reached Ubulun, thirty miles from Urga. Late that night their patrols captured two motor-cars full of Jewish refugees, including a businessman with a Swiss passport, who were making a belated dash for the border. 'All', we are told, 'were lynched with great gaiety.' The same night Colonel Hiroyama, who had been commanding a Japanese detachment serving with the Baron, managed to escape and make his way to Urga to give himself up. But this did not worry the Baron, who simply sent a message to his Chinese enemies to warn them that he was really a Russian spy, with the result that on his arrival in Urga the colonel was immediately executed.

Before launching his third attack on the Holy City, Ungern, in the hope of saving ammunition and gaining some recruits, sent an ultimatum calling on the Chinese garrison to surrender and offering to enrol them in his army. But this they rejected out of hand and retaliated by arresting all the Russians in Urga, looting the Russian Cathedral and Consulate and fining the Living Buddha 200,000 dollars. Preparations for the attack now began in earnest, and soon the lama soothsayers were busier than ever with their dried mutton-bones. A Colonel Dubovik, who, in his simple military way, had actually prepared a detailed plan of attack, was laughed out of court.

But the Baron's plans, by whatever means they were evolved, did not in the event prove unsuccessful. The attack was due to go in on the night of 31 January–1 February. It was bitterly cold. As a first step the Baron gave orders for small groups of men to light big fires in the hills above Urga, so as to make the enemy think that his troops were more numerous than in fact they were. This stratagem worked so well that the Chinese, despite their greatly superior numbers, actually sent off a messenger across a thousand miles of Gobi to Peking to beg for reinforcements. While the main body of the Baron's troops made a direct attack on the Chinese barracks, a smaller force of about 300 men, including sixty Tibetans, were to climb the thickly wooded sacred mountain of Bogdo Ul to the south of the city and, taking the enemy in the rear, set free the Living Buddha from his palace, which was now in the hands of the Chinese. Meanwhile a third force of 350 men were to block the Chinese line of retreat by the caravan route across the Gobi to Kaljan.

By midnight the Baron's troops were in position, but the attack was delayed by the late arrival of the three or four guns mounted on ox-carts which constituted his artillery, and so did not go in until dawn. Thus the element of surprise was lost and the whole force at once came under heavy fire from the Chinese. It was, however, essential that, come what might, the Living Buddha should be liberated on the appointed day and the old prophecy fulfilled. It was also most important for the success of the whole enterprise that the Baron should get the Living Buddha into his own hands without delay. Accordingly, while the other two groups made a strong frontal attack on the Chinese positions, the special raiding party climbed the sacred mountain, burst into the palace, seized the Bogda Gegen, and, bundling the blind old man on to a horse between those of two Tibetan lamas, galloped away with him as fast as they could.

In the course of these engagements, the 12,000 Chinese defenders suffered very heavy casualties and also lost a good number of guns, machine-guns and ammunition, which were promptly turned against them by the Baron's troops. By midday a couple of thousand Chinese had taken to their heels and the remainder had barricaded themselves as best they could into several buildings in the centre of the city, notably the Bulun Barracks, the Russian Consulate, and the solidly built offices of the Russian Goldmining Company.

For the Baron victory was now assured. But it was still only the first of February, and according to the latest prophecies the right date for his actual victory was the third. He accordingly disengaged and spent the rest of the day regrouping his forces and strengthening his positions. But that same night, while they were waiting for another forty-eight hours to elapse, one of his men happened by chance to fire a rocket into the sky. Whereupon the Chinese, not knowing what was happening, opened up with everything they had and the Baron's troops, impatient for action, at once advanced to the attack without waiting for orders. At this the Baron, carried away by the same impulse, mounted his horse and rushed to the head of his troops to lead the attack, galloping as hard as he could go straight at the enemy's barbed wire. Soon his men were in amongst the Chinese, bayoneting them where they stood, while the Cossacks attacked them from the rear. In the savage street-fighting that followed the attackers blew in the doors and windows of the houses with hand-grenades and then set fire to the buildings. Before long the battle had become a massacre and the whole town was given over to murder and looting by the Baron's victorious army.

A participant has left a lively account of the proceedings: 'Mad with revenge and hatred, the conquerors began plundering the city. Drunken horsemen galloped along the streets shooting and killing at their fancy, dragging things outside into the filthy streets, dressing themselves in rich silks found in the shops. In front of the Chinese banks lines were formed. Each man was allowed to plunge his bloody hands into the safes and take out what his luck brought him. Some were lucky enough to pull out gold coins and bullion. Some were less fortunate and only got silver. Jokes and laughter drowned the noise of the fighting. There were some remarkable scenes, too, when the Chinese prisons were opened and the Russian prisoners set free. Crazed by hunger, they threw themselves on any food they could find, tearing raw meat with their teeth like wild beasts. Mad with joy, they kissed all the horsemen within reach. Led by Dr Klingenberg, the Baron's chief medical officer, the mob now attacked the Jews and all of them perished in agony. The humiliation of the women was so awful that I saw one of the officers run inside a house with a razor and offer to let a girl commit suicide before she was attacked. With tears of gratitude she thanked him in a few simple words and then cut her throat ... The drunken mob invented a new sport, which consisted of killing people in the streets by hitting them in the face with thick wooden blocks. One Cossack was killing his own men left and right until someone shot him. Cadet Smirnov chose to strangle old ladies, because he enjoyed seeing them wriggle as he broke their necks. Mr Olsen, a Dane, was dragged along the streets by a rope tied to a wild horse until he was dead. Many women offered to sell themselves to save the lives of their husbands and brothers. But, as often as not, they were cheated in the end ...'

At first the Mongols had welcomed Baron Ungern and his men as liberators. It was not long before they discovered their mistake. Entering Urga at the head of his victorious army, into which he had managed to instil a measure of discipline by dint of massive floggings and executions, the Baron, on whom the Living Buddha had by now obligingly bestowed the exalted title of Khan, at once announced his intention of liquidating all those who had had any dealings either with the Chinese or with the Bolsheviks — in short the greater part of the population. At the same time the Living Buddha, 'a stout old man with a heavy shaven face resembling those of the Cardinals of Rome' and 'wide-open, blind eyes', was proclaimed Emperor of All Mongolia, with Ungern doubling the roles of Military Adviser and God of War.

The Baron now instituted a reign of terror for which it would be hard to find a parallel, and which he only interrupted for occasional sorties against such Chinese as still remained in the country. Contemporary accounts abound in tales of baker's boys being baked alive in their own ovens; of sacks filled with human ears; of elderly Tartars driven up on the roofs of their homes in midwinter and kept dancing there like madmen to stop themselves freezing to death; of young women being raped to death by whole squadrons of Mongol cavalrymen; of Jews having water poured over them till their arms or legs froze stiff and could be snapped off at will; of prisoners being fed to the Baron's private pack of wolves; of innumerable men, women and children of all ages, races and creeds being hacked to bits and bayoneted and shot and strangled and hung and crucified and burnt alive, whenever possible in the presence of the Baron himself, who, we are told, watched their widely varying death struggles with glee, though, when it came to the point, his 'favourite and most-used penalty was lashing to death.'

By all accounts most of the men around Ungern seem to have shared his tastes and inclinations. His adjutant Ensign Burdukovski, otherwise known as Teapot, is described as 'the gayest of the murderers', a 'huge powerful animal', who was always present when Ungern received a visitor. Tall and heavily built, he had a vast body, deep-chested with massive arms and legs. His little curly blond head rested on broad shoulders. His small colourless blue eyes, cold and expressionless, looked out from under a low, narrow forehead. His tiny nose was lost in a flat face. His wide mouth, with its thick, fleshy lips, remained rigid. When he spoke, he did so contemptuously through his teeth out of one corner of his mouth. He had, too, a distressing habit of whistling tunelessly through his teeth on a single note. His unusual nickname had not been idly given. Should the Baron in the course of an interview ask for 'a teapot', Burdukovski knew exactly what to do. Cautiously, he would approach the visitor from behind and then suddenly strangle him to death with his powerful hands.

By some authorities, notably Dr Ossendowski, Colonel Sepailov, for a time the commandant of Urga, is represented as Baron Ungern's evil genius, 'the darkest person on the canvas of Mongolian events', 'the inventive genius of the most outrageous murders'. Short and bald, with a strangely shaped skull beneath his green peaked uniform cap, 'always nervously jerking and wriggling his body and talking ceaselessly, making most un-attractive sounds in his throat and sputtering with saliva all over his lips, his whole face often contracted with spasms', the Colonel cannot have been a pretty sight. Though usually accompanied by two professional execu-tioners, he preferred, we are told, to carry out as many executions as possible himself, singing and joking as he performed the grisly task. He had, it appears a score to pay off against the Bolsheviks, who had murdered his whole family in cold blood, and this made his task a particularly enjoyable one when it came to dispatching Soviet prisoners. Even the Baron became uneasy at his excesses, and twice appointed a commission of surgeons to examine him in the hope that they would prescribe a rest-cure. But Sepailov countered by finding a witch-doctor in Transbaikalia who prophesied that the Baron would die if he ever dispensed with his services, and thus successfully secured his own continued employment.

Another killer was General Rezhukin, the Commander of the Tartar Division, small in his torn grey Mongol coat and old green Cossack cap, 'the dirtiest human being I ever saw,' with a soft voice and courteous manner. He is described as 'the Baron's watchdog, ready to throw himself into the fire or spring at the throat of anyone his master might indicate'. A man of 'absolute bravery and boundless cruelty', the other officers were terrified of him. General Rezhukin's adjutant was Captain Veselosvki, a tall young man with long curly red hair and an unusually white face, heavy and stolid with large steel-cold eyes and beautiful, tender, almost girlish lips. 'In his eyes', we are told, 'there was such cold cruelty that it was quite unpleasant to look at his otherwise fine face.'

By comparison with these, Colonel Kazagrandi, the commander of another White Russian force, which had somehow found its way into Mongolia, was almost normal. 'Strong and handsome', Italian by origin, he fancied himself as a Cossack and modelled himself on the legendary Cossack leader Stenka Razin, responding readily when those around him played the popular tune associated with his hero.

Finally there was Djambolon, a Buriat Mongol, who had fought along-side the Baron on the German front. A simple shepherd, middle-aged and tall, with a long thin face, he was descended from the old Buriat kings and was an expert soothsayer. As such, he became the Baron's treasurer and most trusted personal adviser, scanning the cracks in the mutton-bones and helping the Baron to dispose his troops in accordance with them, but, as

Outer Mongolia

Ulan Bator: the main square

◀ Lighting up

Mother and child

Ulan Bator   At the polls

◄ At the circus

At the Gandang Monastery

The Chief Lama and some of his clergy

One of the Terrible Gods ▶

Dromedaries

A herdsm

Mongolia

A horseman ▶

Lining up the family

Waiting for the kettle to boil

The lady of the *ger*

The lasso

A boy and his horse

The Monastery of Erdeni Tsu

A lama ▶

Kara Korum

the campaign wore on, ever more inclined to prophesy doom. 'I see the God of War', screamed one of the soothsayers he called in, as she twitched and writhed in a self-induced trance. 'His life runs out ... horribly ... After it a shadow, black like the night. Beyond, darkness ... nothing ... ' And the Baron, for once, seemed disturbed by what he had heard.

Ungern's easy victory at Urga had gone to his head. Confirmed in his belief that he was a military genius with a divinely ordained mission, he now decided to extend his operations across the border into Russian territory, where he was convinced that the population, groaning under Bolshevik oppression, would flock in their thousands to join him in his triumphal march on Moscow.

The Bolsheviks for their part were by now becoming seriously disturbed at the Baron's activities. Towards the end of 1920, after Ungern's first attack on Urga, Sukhe Bator and his companions had left Irkutsk and moved to the Mongolian frontier near Kyakhta, where they set about organizing a revolutionary party and government in exile. On 1 March 1921, after the Baron's successful occupation of Urga, the first Congress of the newly formed Mongolian People's Party was held in Kyakhta, and it was decided to form a Mongolian People's Government and raise a National Army to free the country both from the Chinese and from the Baron. On 19 March the formation of the new government was announced, with Sukhe Bator as Prime Minister and Minister of War, and the help of the Red Army was formally invoked against Ungern.

But the Baron decided to strike first, and, having by one method or another assembled several thousand more recruits, prepared to launch a full-scale offensive northwards into Soviet territory. His hope was that his former commander, Hetman Semyonov, and two other surviving Tsarist generals would at the same time strike westwards with such forces as they still had. Before leaving Urga, Ungern issued a final order of the day, proclaiming the Grand Duke Michael Emperor of all the Russias, announcing that it was his intention 'to exterminate commissars, communists and Jews with their families', declaring that 'in this struggle against the criminal destroyers and defilers of Russia, the punishment can only be one: the death penalty in various degrees'; rejecting 'former foreign allies who are suffering from the same revolutionary disease'; and concluding with a somewhat obscure quotation from the Book of Daniel, predicting the appearance of 'Michael the Great Prince' and ending with the words 'Blessed is he that waiteth and cometh to the thousand three hundred and five and thirty days.'

Meanwhile for twenty thousand Mexican dollars the Baron had hired seven thousand lamas to invoke divine intervention on his behalf. His manner by now had become increasingly apocalyptic. He was haunted by ever more insistent premonitions of impending doom and spent more and more of his time careering across country at night in an immense open Fiat touring car with blaring horn and glaring headlights.

After a final review of his troops, the Baron set out from Urga on 27 May, leaving orders with Sepailov for all remaining Russians to be slaughtered so that no witnesses of his reign of terror should survive. Soviet head-quarters were at this time at Verkhneudinsk, and with his main force he now struck northwards along the road from Urga to Troitskosavsk, with the object of cutting the railway line between Irkutsk and eastern China. This, he calculated, would stop the Bolsheviks from bringing up supplies and reserves and make it possible for him to seize and hold the country to the east of the railway.

But this time things did not go according to plan. On reaching Kyakhta, he found that one of his columns, the Chahar Division, under the command of the Mongol Prince Bayer Gun, had engaged the enemy prematurely and been heavily defeated. He also learned that the wounded were receiving inadequate attention. His reaction was immediate. In a rage, he grabbed his Chief Medical Officer, Dr Klingenberg, a 'long-faced aristocrat' with a reputation for poisoning his patients, and, in the words of an onlooker, 'threw him to the ground and beat him with his bamboo until the doctor's legs were broken and he was a complete wreck'. 'Thus', observes the on-looker sadly, 'the only available medical assistance was destroyed at the very beginning of the campaign.' He next sent for Prince Puntzuk, the Governor of the Bangar Kure Province. Once again we have a first-hand account of what ensued. 'When the Prince arrived, he could not but ex-press his doubts in regard to combating the regular army of Bolsheviks which was equipped with all the machinery of modern war: the Baron was enraged and ordered the Prince to be buried alive. Which was done.'

With the main body of his troops Ungern now pushed on into Soviet territory and attacked and occupied the first village he came to. He had ex-pected the peasants to welcome him as a liberator, but, instead, most of them fled from him in terror. Furious, he assembled as many as he could find in a large barn and gave orders for them to be burnt alive, while he himself said a prayer to Buddha.

Instead of making the most of the advantage he had gained and pressing

on to Verkhneudinsk, the Baron, after a brush with a Soviet detachment and
a long, hard look at the mutton-bones, now lingered for three days at
Keran. On the fourth day the Red Cavalry attacked him in strength and a
fierce battle ensued. After six hours of incessant fighting, the Soviet troops
withdrew into the nearby forest and the Baron's troops followed them.
This was what the Soviet commander had hoped for. No sooner had the
Baron's men entered the forest than they came under a strong concentration of artillery and machine-gun fire, which ploughed into their ranks
with devastating effect. Not until late that night were they able to fight their
way out of the trap.

Next morning the Baron ordered the survivors to march on Kyakhta,
some six or seven miles away. But, before they could move, the enemy
attacked them again from three sides. Seeing that they were about to be
surrounded, as many as could dropped everything and made for the hills,
leaving behind their arms, ammunition, food and medical supplies. Even
the Baron, who had himself been wounded in the fighting, seemed dis-
couraged, as well he might. 'It is remarkable', writes an eye-witness, 'how
little strategy the Baron knew. He was defeated by a much weaker oppo-
nent who had only half as much artillery and half as many men.'

After this setback, there was nothing for it but to retreat into Mongolia.
On reaching the Orkhon River, after a painful withdrawal through difficult
country, the Baron received fresh reinforcements in the shape of two
Mongolian regiments from Urga. 'The Baron', we are told, 'recovered his
self confidence again. He hanged Colonel Arhipov ... and burned alive Dr
Engelgard-Escrski.' A new arrival named Petkovski 'was so horrified at
seeing a living man broiled that he jumped into the river and drowned
himself'. By now the saying 'Rather Death than the Baron' was on the lips
of more and more people. Many endured both.

Having first dispatched his captured valuables under escort to Uliassutai
and dumped all his silver at the bottom of the Orkhon River near the
Erdeni Dzu Monastery, where silver was traditionally deposited as a
tribute to the Spirit of the River, Ungern now once more resumed the
offensive, advancing along the Selenga River to the south of Lake Baikal
and then turning east in the direction of Verkhneudinsk. This time he was
more successful, defeating two strong Soviet units which were sent to meet
him. His troops massacred all the prisoners they took. 'The Red nurses',
we are told, 'were given to soldiers hungry for women's bodies. All died
during the endless humiliation.'

But for Baron Ungern the day of reckoning was at hand. He now learned that three Soviet cavalry regiments were closing in on him from the north and three from the east, while to the south his retreat was cut off by the crack Shetinkin Sharpshooters. The battle lasted for two days and nights, the Baron's troops holding out as long as they could, in the hope that Hetman Semyonov and the other two Tsarist generals in the neighbourhood might come to their rescue. But Semyonov, seeing that this time the Bolsheviks meant business, kept out of their way and eventually saved his own skin by withdrawing into Manchuria.* And in the end Ungern's army, defenceless against the aircraft the enemy were now using against them, fell back once more into Mongolia, as usual looting and massacring as they went.

Meanwhile the Reds were fast spreading out over Mongolia, taking one place after another. In the circumstances the Baron decided to march with such troops as remained to him in the direction of Muren Kure, *en route*, if he could reach it, for Chuguchak in Chinese Turkestan, where it was said that Russian officers were earning their keep by selling their wives to the Chinese. His troops, even the Cossacks, were now deserting in ever larger numbers. The country through which he passed was empty, the inhabitants having very sensibly gone into hiding. 'The Baron', writes one of his officers, 'rode silently with bowed head in front of the column. He had lost his hat and most of his clothes. On his naked chest numerous Mongolian talismans and different charms hung on a bright yellow cord. He looked like the reincarnation of a prehistoric ape-man. People were afraid even to look at him.'

When they were still seventy miles short of Muren Kure, the news reached them that it had already been taken by the enemy. Strong Soviet forces were also closing in on them from the rear. Again they were in danger of being trapped. Ungern's officers, who had finally lost confidence in him, now sent two of their number to General Rezhukhin to suggest that he should assume command. Rezhukhin's answer was to have them both soundly flogged — one hundred strokes apiece. But by now things had gone too far. A night or two later one of the supposedly more reliable units suddenly opened up with a machine-gun at Rezhukhin's tent. Rezhukhin was wounded and, just as one of his officers was tying up his wounds, a Cossack crept up on them from behind and shot the General dead.

That same night a Colonel Evforitski ordered his machine-gunners to open fire on Baron Ungern's tent. After several bursts, the Baron came out,

---

*Where, as things turned out, he was to meet his end at the hands of the same Red Army a quarter of a century later, at the end of World War II.

jumped on his horse and galloped off into the night. The gigantic Ensign Burdukovski, who now appeared on the scene, was cut down by a Cossack with his sabre and then shot dead. Then suddenly the Baron himself returned to the camp and faced the mutineers. Such was the hold he still had over them that at first they all stood rooted to the ground, not knowing what to do. Then an officer, Captain Makeyev, pulled out his revolver and fired it at him, and again the Baron galloped off into the darkness. First to the Buriats: but they opened fire on him. Then to his Mongols: but they, too, were hostile. By now Ungern was losing a lot of blood from his wounds, and in the end fell unconscious from his horse. Meanwhile the mutiny had taken hold and on every side old scores were being settled as informers and executioners were hacked to pieces by infuriated Cossacks. Once some sort of order had been restored, a Colonel Kostromin took command, re-formed the Russian units and marched them off to the Chinese border and to exile. The Baron they simply left to his fate.

Even now Baron Ungern presented a problem for the Mongols who found him where he lay. Their belief that he was indeed Tzagan Burkhan, the God of War, and consequently immortal, had been reinforced by the events of the night. Had not everyone tried to shoot him? And was he not still alive? After much deliberation a number of their bravest men were sent with ropes to bind him hand and foot. When they had done this, they galloped off, each in a different direction, before the divine wrath could overtake them.

Next day a Red patrol, happening to pass through the valley, came upon a solitary, helpless, shackled figure, lying in the grass with the ants running over him. 'Who are you, stranger?' they asked. 'I', came the angry answer in the famous high-pitched tenor, 'am Baron Ungern-Sternberg.'

Such was the terror the Baron inspired that the first impulse of the Red soldiers who had found him was to turn tail and run. But then, pulling themselves together, they picked him up, brushed the ants off him, gave him a drink and took him back with them to their headquarters.

The capture of the notorious Baron Ungern naturally caused a considerable stir in Bolshevik circles, and we are told that he was taken to Verkhneudinsk 'in a private first-class Pullman car'. According to one story, an attempt was made to induce him to join the Red Army, where it was perhaps felt that he might have his uses. But, if that attempt was indeed made, nothing came of it, and in due course the Baron was brought to trial and, not surprisingly, sentenced to death and shot.

15 *People's Republic*

On 6 July 1921 the Red Army, together with Sukhe Bator's new National Army, occupied Urga, and five days later established there a new Mongolian National Government, with Sukhe Bator as Minister of War and a lama called Bodo as Prime Minister. For the time being the Living Buddha remained Head of State, but with functions that were in the main religious. In response to a request from the new Mongolian Government, the Soviet Government agreed to leave their troops in Mongolia for as long as they were needed, and on 5 November 1921 a Treaty of Friendship was signed between the two countries. In April 1922 Bodo, together with ten other leading Mongols, was executed on a charge of conspiring with the Chinese and Sukhe Bator succeeded him as Prime Minister. In short, despite everything that had happened during the intervening period both in Russia and in Mongolia, the situation was once again not so very different from that established six years earlier by the Tsarist Government under the Treaty of Kyakhta.

Later in 1922, at the Independence Day celebrations, young Sukhe Bator the Liberator delighted the crowd by galloping at full tilt down the field and leaning as he did so from the saddle to pick up silver dollars from the ground. He was a leader after their own hearts. A year later he was dead, poisoned, it was said, by a lama doctor.

The following year saw the death of the Living Buddha after a primacy of nearly half a century, an event of which the new People's Government took advantage to announce that, in accordance with an ancient prophecy, there would be no further reincarnations of the Living Buddha of Urga. 'Buddha's will', ran the Government proclamation, 'has been fulfilled. The spirit of the Bogda Gegen, after his eighth reincarnation, has gone to Nirvana and will not return again.' After which Outer Mongolia was once and for all declared a People's Republic and became the first, and for many years the only, Soviet satellite.

Though their country had now officially ceased to be a theocracy, the problems confronting the Marxists of the New Mongolia were manifold.

There were no towns and there was no industry. There was therefore no urban or industrial proletariat. There was little or no trade and therefore no native bourgeoisie or commercial class. There was no agriculture and therefore, strictly speaking, no landowners or peasants. In effect, apart from the lamas, the whole population were nomads and herdsmen, a few of their leaders enjoying various vague feudal rights and bearing hereditary titles of nobility. In short, it was not at all the sortof society that Karl Marx had had in mind when he wrote *Das Kapital*.

Lenin, who was believed by some to have Mongol blood himself, gave it as his view that the Mongols, as a race of herdsmen and nomads, would do well to go slow and approach Socialism in the first place by starting co-operatives. And this, at varying rates of progress, and with varying degrees of success and various deviations to Right and Left, duly followed by purges of the offending deviationists, they have been trying to do ever since. From 1932 until 1952, a period roughly corresponding, in more respects than one, to the Stalin era in Russia, Mongolia was firmly ruled by Sukhe Bator's fellow revolutionary, Marshal Choibalsan. During this period there were no deviations, only some purges and what is now regarded, not without hindsight, as a somewhat exaggerated cult of personality. On Choibalsan's death his place was taken by Mr Yumzhagin Tsedenbal, another dependable ally of the Soviet Union, who at the time of writing is still in power, conveniently combining the offices of Prime Minister and Party Secretary.

Today, more than fifty years after the Revolution, Mongolia is still basically a nation of nomads and herdsmen. But during the last twenty years things have been moving apace in a number of different directions.

The power of the lamas has long since been broken. Now only two or three monasteries remain open, and there are not more than a couple of hundred lamas all told. At the Gandang Monastery in Ulan Bator, once the seat of the Living Buddha, and now one of the few religious centres still in use, we watched the lamas at their devotions, heard them blow their trumpets, clash their cymbals and beat their drums, while outside a number of worshippers prostrated themselves on prayer-boards especially provided for that purpose. After the service we took tea in a comfortable ceremonial tent with the Abbot, an affable old gentleman with charming manners wearing fine scarlet robes. But apart from this we were to detect but few signs of life from a once all-powerful Church.

Modern education and a modern health service (partly airborne) have made considerable progress. Illiteracy has been practically eliminated, and many of the diseases which were rampant forty or fifty years ago have been stamped out. The population is now well into its second million and growing fast. In the technical and scientific field the Mongols have shown themselves quick to learn, and foreign instructors have by now in the main made way for their former pupils. Already there are thousands of students in higher institutions, and a Mongolian doctor can now complete his whole training without ever leaving his own country.

Near Ulan Bator coal is mined on a large scale and elsewhere copper, gold and iron ore are also being worked. Round Sain Shanda, in the Gobi, oil has been struck, and in other parts of the country other industrial centres and settlements are springing up. Finally, the railway now links Ulan Bator directly with Moscow and Peking.

But stock-breeding and livestock-rearing remain the basis of the Mongolian economy. With getting on for 25 million head of livestock to a human population of not much more than a million, Mongolia has the highest *per capita* rate of livestock in the world. Of these roughly 80 per cent are sheep and goats, 10 per cent cattle and yaks, 8 per cent horses, and 2 per cent camels. Having failed disastrously to induce the Mongolian arats or herdsmen to accept collectivization in the late 'twenties and early 'thirties, the authorities prudently let the matter rest until 1957, when an intensive new collectivization campaign met with greater success. Today, practically 100 per cent of the arats are members of ever-larger *negdels* or co-operatives, and there are also thirty or more large state farms, owning herds of their own. At several of these we were plied with food and drink and endless statistics, and shown such farming operations as were in progress.

Collectivization has, however, altered the life of the average Mongolian herdsman less than one might think. Part of the livestock is still privately owned by the members of each co-operative, and apart from technical and scientific progress in the field of animal husbandry and veterinary science, there has been little change in the traditional pattern of their existence. Each negdel now has its permanent administrative and social headquarters complete with school and hospital, but round these herds and herdsmen continue their nomadic peregrinations, as the season and the state of their allotted pastures demand. Now, as always, the arat's home remains his circular *ger*. It is here that he and his family are born, live and die. It is here, too, that the traveller, wherever he comes from, will find a friendly welcome and lavish hospitality.

What may in the long run have more effect on Mongolian life is the introduction of arable farming. For centuries the Mongols were opposed to disturbing the soil and its spirits on religious grounds, and as recently as 1929 only 8,000 acres were under cultivation in the whole country, and these almost entirely by Chinese. In 1959, however, a ploughing programme on the enormous scale of Khrushchev's Virgin Lands project was undertaken by a number of state farms and co-operatives. This bold experiment proved on the whole successful, and by 1961 for the first time the Mongols were able to supply their own requirements of wheat and to export some as well.

Today Mongolia strikes one as a prosperous enough country. People are on the whole well fed and well dressed, whether in the traditional Mongol *del* or in European clothes. Cars are not as yet very numerous, but bicycles and motor-bicycles are beginning to make their appearance, and there is always a horse for everyone. In the shops in Ulan Bator there are plenty of consumer goods, imported for the most part from Russia or China or from the other Communist countries.

Politically, Mongolia has much in common with any other Communist state. 'What', the Mongols asked me after a tour of elaborately insulated polling-booths on election day, 'do you think of our elections?' 'Admirable', I replied, 'except that you have only one party.' And yet it would be a mistake to assume that Mongolia is no more than an outlying province of the Soviet Empire. Fifty years after the Red Army helped Sukhe Bator to liquidate the Mad Baron, the Mongolian People's Republic gives in many ways a greater impression of independence than do some Communist countries in Eastern Europe.

One reason for this, I suspect, is that the Mongols are so intensely proud of everything Mongolian. For men and women alike the brightly coloured traditional Mongol robe, or *del*, which is both practical and ornamental, still predominates over European dress. On every occasion brimming silver bowls of *airag* are handed round in preference to Crimean port or Caucasian champagne. And, when summer comes, even the occupants of the most luxurious apartments in Ulan Bator pack their *gers* into a truck or on to a camel and take to the hills or plains. Likewise the Three Manly Sports – Horsemanship, Wrestling and Archery – still hold the same place in Mongol life as they did in the days of Jenghiz Khan.

Wrestling, in particular, is tremendously important. The day we arrived the stands all round the great arena were packed with an immense, noisy crowd. The sun shone; bright blue and vermilion banners flapped in the wind. Everyone in the crowd knew every hold and throw, and even the little children could be seen practising them on the side-lines, all aspiring in due course to the titles of Lion, Elephant or Eagle awarded to the national champions. As one pair of contestants after another flapped out on to the field in their traditional eagle dance, and then went into a series of steadily maintained clinches interspersed by sudden bouts of violent action, excitement gradually rose, and even the ceremonially dressed heralds or seconds, who circle round holding the wrestlers' hats, joined in with encouraging slaps and cries. Then when, after much straining and manœuvring, one or other contestant had lost his balance and been thrown, the winner, flapping his arms like an eagle's wings, went into his victory dance; the crowd yelled with excitement; and the next round started. Out in the middle of the field, completely absorbed with my task of filming, I found myself again and again about to become mixed up in one or other of the contests. Meanwhile in tents and booths all round the ground, *airag* was flowing freely as the finer points of each match were discussed by everyone from the Prime Minister downwards.

Watching this, or watching the mares being milked or a string of camels moving across the plain, or watching a couple of herdsmen single out a horse from the herd, hunt it at full gallop in and out of several hundred stampeding mares and stallions, lasso it, bring it down, saddle it, mount it and, after much bucking and kicking, ride it to a standstill, it was quite easy to forget all the new government offices and factories and apartment houses of Ulan Bator and feel transported to a heroic, Homeric age.

What, I wondered, as I climbed on to the train for Peking, does the future hold for Mongolia? With her recognition, first by the various Communist countries of the world and latterly by a number of non-Communist countries, and with her entry to the United Nations, Mongolia has finally emerged from her long isolation and is ready to play her part in world affairs. This is bound to be to some extent conditioned by her geographical situation. Wedged between China and the Soviet Union, Mongolia seems unlikely to stray far from Communism of one kind or another. But with the progressive deterioration of Sino-Soviet relations, her position has of late gained a fresh significance, at the moment underlined by the presence in Mongolia of substantial numbers of Soviet troops.

For years, while maintaining relations with both, the Mongolian Government have made it clear that their sympathies lie with the Russians. The reasons for this are not far to seek. In the past Mongolia has looked to Russia for help and found it. What is more, she is still finding it in the shape of substantial economic aid. Even today 75 per cent of Mongolia's trade is still with Russia. She is a full member of Comecon, and Russia grants her lavish loans and credit.

For a time Mongolia also received aid from China, but on a smaller scale and mainly in the form of direct Chinese labour. Moreover, the anxiety of the Chinese to send thousands of blue-clad labourers to build roads and blocks of flats for the Mongolians was in itself a reminder that China, with her fast-expanding population, already running at 700 million and likely to reach 1,000 million by the end of the century, must in the natural course of events be looking for somewhere for all those millions to expand into. And where more convenient then the neighbouring plains of Mongolia, with their largely untapped resources? Nor can either race forget the centuries when the whole of Mongolia was part of China, or forget that Inner Mongolia is already an integral part of the Chinese People's Republic and heavily colonized by Chinese settlers.

For all these reasons the Mongols' preference for Moscow is readily understandable. But, though in foreign policy the Mongolian Government regularly follow the Soviet line, there is little or no indication of Russification or of active Soviet interference in Mongolian internal affairs. Indeed, the continued presence of large statues of Generalissimo Stalin all over Ulan Bator long after de-Stalinization was an accomplished fact in the Soviet Union in itself pointed to a certain political independence.

Without for a moment suggesting that the Mongols would do anything so indelicate as to play one Communist colossus off against the other, it is conceivable that they may find certain tactical advantages in their delicately poised position between the two. And now, with the opening up of new contacts with the outside world, all kinds of fresh possibilities are fast emerging.

For almost a century now, despite world wars, revolutions, and numerous other alarms and excursions, the frontiers of empire in Central Asia have stayed largely undisturbed. What are the prospects of their remaining so in the future?

Of the empires once involved, one, our own, has faded more or less gracefully from the scene, leaving in the Indian sub-continent a situation of considerable potential instability. The Russians and Chinese, on the other hand, have both emerged from the trials and ordeals of the last fifty years much strengthened and refreshed, and, though both nominally of the same ideological persuasion, today confront each other uneasily across several thousand miles of frontier, a frontier which the Chinese, for their part, openly declare their reluctance to accept as final. Across this frontier, meanwhile, a frightening imbalance is building up between, on the one hand, the vast empty plains and abundant, scarcely tapped, resources of Siberia, Mongolia and Kazakstan and, on the other, the busy, teeming millions of Chinese, an imbalance which even the most detached observer could hardly fail to find disturbing.

South of the Himalayas, moreover, in the former territories of the British Raj, Chinese and Russians now both have their own allies, who in their turn regard each other with barely veiled hostility. And what our grandfathers called the Great Game is played today with different pieces on another board. Nor, looking back over two or three thousand years of Central Asian history, is it possible to leave entirely out of account those sudden mysterious urges and impulses which have always swayed races and peoples one way or another and caused them to invade this or that territory or to rebel against this or that allegiance or creed. Historically speaking, there can be no doubt that both Russians and Chinese have ample reason for looking at their neighbours askance.

And so, day and night for thousands of miles on either side of their common border, Chinese and Soviet frontier guards watch each other warily, while in the pigeon-holes of Moscow and Peking lie contingency plans calculated, it must be assumed, to counter almost any emergency — an emergency which, one must hope, will never in fact arise.

Index of Names